HEARTLANDERS

STEPHEN BILL

Stephen Bill was born and brought up in Handsworth, Birmingham. He was Resident Writer at the Sheffield Crucible in 1978/9 and has since written extensively for stage and television including *The Old Order*, which won the John Whiting Award in 1979. *Piggy Back Riders* (1981), *Naked in the Bull Ring* (1985), *Eh, Brian It's a Whopper* (Central TV Series, 1984), *Marjorie and the Preacher Man* (BBC-TV, 1987, co-written with Jim Broadbent) and *Crossing the Line* (1987). He won both the Evening Standard and the Plays and Players Most Promising Playwright Award in 1987 for *Curtains*, which also won the Drama Magazine Best Play Award.

ANNE DEVLIN

Anne Devlin was born in Belfast and now lives in Birmingham. She has written four screenplays for the BBC, including *Naming the Names*, which won the 8th International Celtic Film Festival Prize, and *The Venus de Milo Instead*, winner of the San Francisco Film and Television Best Drama Award. Her stage play, *Ourselves Alone*, won both the George Devine Award and the Susan Blackburn Prize in 1986. She adapted D.H. Lawrence's *The Rainbow* for BBC-TV (1988) and has published *The Way-Paver*, a book of short stories.

DAVID EDGAR

David Edgar was born in Birmingham in 1948. Since his first play, the group-written *England's Ireland* (1972), he has written over 20 stage plays, amongst them *Destiny* (John Whiting Award 1976), *The Jail Diary of Albie Sachs* (1978), an adaptation of *Nicholas Nickleby* (1980, which won SWET and New York Tony Awards) and *Maydays* (Plays and Players Best Play Award 1983), all premiered by the RSC, as well as *Entertaining Strangers* (Dorchester Community Play, 1985, National Theatre, 1987). He wrote the 1986 film, *Lady Jane*, directed by Trevor Nunn and *Vote for Them* for BBC-TV (1989). From autumn 1989, he chairs Britain's first MA in playwriting, at Birmingham University.

STEPHEN BILL
ANNE DEVLIN
DAVID EDGAR

HEARTLANDERS

A community play to celebrate
Birmingham's centenary

NICK HERN BOOKS

A division of Walker Books Limited

A Nick Hern Book

Heartlanders first published in 1989 as an original paperback by
Nick Hern Books, a division of Walker Books Limited, 87 Vauxhall
Walk, London SE11 5HJ

Front cover illustration: Spaghetti Junction
© The Telegraph Colour Library

Set in ITC New Baskerville and printed in Great Britain by
Expression Printers Limited, London N7 9DP

British Library Cataloguing in Publication Data

    Bill, Stephen
    Heartlanders.
    I. Title   II. Devlin, Anne
    III. Edgar, David, *1948-*
    822'.914

ISBN 1-85459-086-3

Characters in order of appearance

BA, AAN's mother.
AAN, a young Asian man.
AAN'S BROTHER.
AIRPORT OFFICIAL.
TOM LLEWELLYN, a white man from Wales.
MARGARET PRICE, a middle-aged white woman.
JOHAN, a Central European music student.
BUS INSPECTOR.
DEPUTY INSPECTOR.
ROSE DEVINE, a young white woman from Ireland.
SISTER CLARE ⎫
SISTER CATHERINE ⎬ nuns.
SISTER MICHAEL ⎪
SISTER MARY ⎭
JOEL, a young Afro-Caribbean man from Birmingham.
RAVI CHATTERJEE, AAN's aunt.
MISH CHATTERJEE, AAN's uncle.
PUSHBA CHATTERJEE, AAN's young cousin.
PETUE, a cab driver (Asian).
ERNEST, a long-haired white man over 30.
NGUGI, JOEL's friend (Afro-Caribbean).
LEARIE, JOEL's friend (Afro-Caribbean).
RECEPTIONIST.
CLAPPER, late teens.
KAREN, late teens, pregnant.
PATRICIA MORRIS, TOM's friend. Originally from Wales.
TERRY, early to mid-thirties, man from Birmingham.
MICHELLE, KAREN's friend.
SHARON, MICHELLE'S friend.
DEBBIE, SHARON's friend.
HENRY ⎫
LYNN ⎬ Yuppie couple.
LUIGI BENNEDOTTI, Pizzeria Manager.
GEORGE JONES ⎫
TED WILSON ⎬ security men.
TRACY, waitress.
TRISHA ⎫
AHMED ⎬ friends of Debbie.
BONES ⎭
REG ⎫
GWEN ⎬ pensioners.
VI ⎭

SOLDIER

WENDY
KELLY } women hairdressers.

KATYA CHATTERJEE, AAN's cousin.

MARTIN MURPHY, KATYA's boyfriend. A young white man from Ireland.

DJ, a young man from Birmingham.

GARY, TRACY's boyfriend.

A CENTURION
INDIAN CHIEF } (Afro-Caribbean or Asian).
INDIAN BRAVE

2 BOUNCERS

MELDIA
MAY } pregnant women.
MRS WHITE

WINSOME.

RITA BRACEBRIDGE, a white woman in her mid to late thirties.

JULIE, a young mother.

WAYNE
LEE } JULIE's children.

ELAINE
CARLA } hairdressing management.
DAVID

FRANCESCA
SUKIE
LULU } computer demonstrators.
MANDIP
CELESTINE

BRENDAN, a catering assistant.

MAGICIAN.

PAM, manageress.

SAMANTHA, hairdresser.

ESTELLE, beautician.

RO, a hairdressing junior.

MRS DYSART, a customer (white).

NURSE, a woman in her early thirties.

KIM, a teacher.

SUE, a teacher.

GABI
DANIEL } children.
ZARA
CONNELL

NORMAN PRICE, MARGARET's husband.

SANDRA PRICE, MARGARET's daughter.

Extras

AAN's family in India (Asian).
Passengers, bus drivers, Polish choir, Welsh choir, ticket clerk at
Bus Station.
Customers, waiters and waitresses at the restaurants.
Dancers, Clint Eastwood Lookalikes at the disco.
Pregnant women at Maternity Hospital.
Children at the playground.
Fire eater, visitors at the NEC.
Doctors, nurses, patients at the casualty unit.
Temple visitors at the Diwalli ceremony (Asian and white).

Cast

Heartlanders is set in the autumn of 1989. The play was first staged at
Birmingham Repertory Theatre on 19 October 1989, with the
following cast:

Sarah Amos
Rhonda Atkins

Peter Banks
Wayne Bradley
Darren Brown
Bob Brown
Stephen Brown
Eileen Budd
Mark Bullock

Suzi Clay
Dawn Clifford
Giovanni Cuccinello
Elizabeth Cureton
Helen Cutler
Mary Cutler

Jeff Dicks
Claire Downes
Eileen Doyle
Martin Doyle

Russell Evans

Shayne Farina
Freyja Fielding
Karen Fisher
Mark Forde
Dawn Foster

June Gabrielle
Lucia Gabrielle
Althea Gaye
Ruth Graham
Margaret Griffiths
Dan Hawthorn
Maria Hesson
David Hill
Hazel Hills
Deborah Hollis
Stanley Holloway
Derek Hunt
Nicola Jones

Manjit Kaur

Arshad Khan

Susan Leighfield

Liz Madeley
Rina Mahoney
Margaret Maloney
Carl Marrey
Pauline Martin
Lynne Matthews
Damien McKeown
Richard Melia
Jackie Moore
Diane Moorecroft

David Nichol

Helen Oakley
Philip O'Neill

Jatinder Pal
Rebecca Palmer
Tania Parker
Kangi Patel
Jennifer Phillips
Jackie Pratt
Lee Priddy
Karen Sayce
Christine Schneider

Denise Seneviratne
James Sherwin
Balkar Singh
Dharmander Singh
Sian Smith
Michael Stewart

Fay Thompson
Richard Thompson
Simone Todd
Kate Tomlinson
Lee Tregellis
Ann Troman
Peter J Tulk
Nicholas Tulloch

Habib Ullah

Mike Venables

Sally Watson
Michael Wilks
Joe White
Stephanie Wright

Robert Yapp
Tony Young

Laura Zimmerman

Director Chris Parr
Set designer Gavin Davies
Costume designer Anne Curry
Music by Peter Graham, Steve Rose
Community Play co-ordinators
Chris Rozanski (Theatre of the Unemployed)
Mick Yates (Birmingham Repertory Theatre)
Assisted by Peter Tulk and Ian Andrews

The workshops for this production were organised by
the Birmingham Repertory Theatre and the Theatre of
the Unemployed.

Note

This script and cast list were correct at the beginning of rehearsals.

ACT ONE

Scene One

AAN's *departure from an airport in India should involve at least ten to twelve people – including children – seeing him off. His mother, father, brother, sisters and grandmother all giving him hugs and advice.*

All this is taking place in front of a poker-faced AIRPORT OFFICIAL *who is waiting to see his passport.*

BA. Speak quietly.

AAN. Yes mother.

BA. Keep your thoughts from your eyes.

AAN. Yes mother.

BA. Guard your back.

AAN. Yes mother.

BA. And always remember, that in the mother's lap the child finds
    every fulfilment.

AAN. Yes mother.

BA. Now your brother has something important to say to you.

    They embrace.

    Goodbye son.

BROTHER. Could you get me a couple of videos?

AAN. I'll see.

EVERYBODY. Goodbye Aan! Bye.

    AAN *moves on to the* AIRPORT OFFICIAL *as the crowd of relatives
    moves off.*

AIRPORT OFFICIAL. How long are you going for?

AAN. Two weeks.

AIRPORT OFFICIAL. I thought you were emigrating!

    He hands AAN *the passport,* AAN *moves away on his own through
    customs.*

Focus shifts to TOM.

TOM. I'll take the Swansea bus from home. Best allow an hour.
Then two o'clock from the bus station. I've got my ticket. I
guess we'll go Neath, Aberdare, Merthyr, the Head of the
Valley to Brynmawr, Abergavenny, Monmouth, up the Wye
valley to Ross then I think it's motorway all the way. Mrs
Pritchard, if you could be so kind – check my letterbox will
you? These bloody free papers you know, they never push
them through . . .

Focus shifts to MARGARET.

MARGARET. Norman. If you've understood the note then you'll be
listening to this tape.

Norman, I have gone away for a few days. There is plenty of
food in the fridge. If you have a problem then Mrs Jackson
could come in tomorrow even though it's her day off and do
for you.

I mean, well, you know what I mean. Her number's Oswestry
653765. But of course you don't dial Oswestry. Because we live
here. Sorry. Silly.

But you shouldn't worry. I'm not 'leaving'. In the sense of
leaving you.

Focus shifts to AAN.

AAN. One day I met a girl on the Beach of Shells and she came
from Birmingham in England – Katya.

Five years is a long time and England is so far – but when I find
her I'm going to walk along a beach in Birmingham. My
mother is afraid to travel: she says the spirit gets confused if
you go to many places and you can lose your spirit in one of
them. Or leave it behind somewhere. I hope I don't lose my
spirit in England.

MARGARET. And I'll be back as soon as I've done what I have to
do.

TOM. No . . . I don't know how long I'll be gone.

Scene Two

Digbeth Bus Station.

Friday. Early evening. Peak time, coaches arriving for the 7 o'clock interchange.

Hundreds of people milling around, struggling with luggage, desperately seeking information from the staff. There are hugs and kisses for people being met. Others search for friends and relatives.

A Welsh male voice choir cuts a swathe through the crowd as they disembark and head with purpose and in full voice for the city centre.

A young, Central European, MUSIC STUDENT, *instrument in hand, stops the* DEPUTY INSPECTOR *as he hurries past.*

JOHAN. Excuse me . . . Please – the school of music?

DEPUTY INSPECTOR. Up the hill, through the market, down the subway, up the steps, down the subway, follow the subway, past Renta Villa, where the toilets used to be, you know? Stay in the subway turn left then ask again.

> *He hurries on leaving the* MUSIC STUDENT *to set off hesitantly in the direction of the subway.*

> *A group of* NUNS *escorts a pregnant teenager towards one of the coaches. This is* ROSE DEVINE. *They are all advising her.*

SISTER CATHERINE. Now the bus doesn't go across the water.

SISTER MICHAEL. So you'll have to get off at Stranraer.

SISTER CLARE. And don't forget to get on the boat!

SISTER MARY. That's very important now! Are you listening?

> ROSE *has spotted a man sitting alone getting his breath back. She breaks away from the sisters and hurries over to him.*

> *He is surprised, but too preoccupied with his breathing to speak. He could be asthmatic. This is* TOM.

ROSE. Uncle! Uncle Bobby what are you doing here? Are you going home? Yes? Yes you are? (*Privately.*) Say you are! There's a coven of witches over there and they're terrorising me!

SISTER MICHAEL. Rose . . .

ROSE. It's all right, this is my uncle!

SISTER MICHAEL. Oh . . .

ROSE. He's going home as well, isn't that good? Well how about that! So that's lovely isn't it? You can all go now, thank you so much! (*To* TOM.) Uncle Bobby well I can't believe it – of all the people . . . and I bet you never expected to see me did you?

It's all right then sisters, thank you so much for your help. I shall write to you and let you know what it is!

SISTER MARY. Oh you must!

SISTER CATHERINE. And is that all right Mr . . .

ROSE. McIlhenney – my dad's brother. He'll look after me, won't you Uncle?

TOM. Listen . . .

ROSE. Shh! Don't you dare! Don't say it! He says terrible things about me so he does! Goodbye then sisters and mind how you go. Keep up the good work now.

She sits down beside TOM.

So Uncle . . .

SISTER CLARE. You'll miss your bus.

ROSE. We won't, we won't! You run along now. (*To* TOM.) How's Aunty Mary and Sean and Danny . . .

SISTER MARY. Well goodbye then . . .

The others all say goodbyes.

ROSE. Bye now and I'll send you the money for the ticket! Thanks ever so much!

They go.

Evil witches! They prey on poor defenceless girls, so they do . . . Anyway, thanks ever so much, you're a pal. I'll see you again maybe. You take care now . . .

She starts to go.

TOM. Heh . . .

ROSE. What?

TOM (*shakes his head*). Are you all right?

ROSE. Of course I am. Are you?

TOM. I'm all right.

ROSE. You could have fooled me.

She offers him her inhaler.

Here have a drag on this . . .

He does so.

TOM. Mine's at the bottom of my case. Thank you.

ROSE. Sorry about that just now. Witches they are. My husband you
see is working in Saudi Arabia and the post, you would not
believe it! His pay cheque just did not come through. I am
skint! So I asked the sisters for help but the minute they put
the ticket in my hand, I thought, oh shit! What am I doing? I'm
not going back to Belfast! Has the Liverpool bus come in yet
do you know?

TOM. I don't know.

ROSE. I'd best away and cash this. Is the ticket office still open do
you know?

TOM. I don't.

ROSE. Thanks anyway. You look after yourself now!

TOM. And you! Hey. Have you ever heard of Castle Bromwich?

TOM *is left alone on the bench. An* INSPECTOR *and* DEPUTY
INSPECTOR *enter, both with clipboards. A young black man,* JOEL,
is trying to attract their attention.

INSPECTOR. Right. If we send out Liverpool then Aberystwyth . . .

DEPUTY INSPECTOR. No, you can't do Aberystwyth.

JOEL. Um, excuse me . . .

INSPECTOR. Why not?

DEPUTY INSPECTOR. Sheffield's 20 minutes over.

INSPECTOR. Don't believe it.

JOEL. S'cuse me, please . . .

DEPUTY INSPECTOR. But if you sent off Liverpool then Bristol
Cardiff Swansea . . .

JOEL. Heathrow?

INSPECTOR. In a moment. Doncaster?

The focus shifts back to TOM, *who has stood to stretch his legs.*

MARGARET *appears.*

MARGARET. Inspector?

TOM. No.

MARGARET. No?

TOM. I'm not the Inspector.

MARGARET. This much is obvious. I wondered if you knew where the Inspector's office was.

TOM. Uh – no. But, isn't that – that man in the blue jacket, with the clipboard . . .

MARGARET. Thank you.

MARGARET *gets to the* INSPECTORS *and* JOEL.

INSPECTOR. All right then. If Sheffield makes it in the next ten minutes, we send out the M5 first and then the M1 and cross-country.

DEPUTY INSPECTOR. Otherwise?

INSPECTOR. We're buggered. They'll just have to take the train.

(*To* JOEL.) Right. What is it?

JOEL. Well . . .

MARGARET *arrives, as the* DEPUTY INSPECTOR *leaves.*

MARGARET. Inspector. I have just arrived from Oswestry.

INSPECTOR. I'm sorry?

JOEL. Uh, excuse me . . .

MARGARET. And I had expected I'd be met. By the police.

JOEL. I mean, you know . . .

INSPECTOR. The police?

MARGARET. That's right.

JOEL. There is a queue.

INSPECTOR. Are you assisting with inquiries?

MARGARET. No I am not. If you want to know, I am looking for a missing person. I have been in contact with the police, and informed them, as they've failed to solve the case, or even frankly made a dent in it as far as I can see, that I would come personally, and that they should meet me here.

INSPECTOR. I see. And this – this person . . . uh, a friend or relative?

MARGARET. Well, it's no concern of yours, but it's my daughter.

INSPECTOR. Ar, well, now, I've got an interchange to manage, here, and in precisely 90 seconds all hell will break loose. But when that's sorted, I'll sort you.

MARGARET. Well, thank you.

INSPECTOR. Right.

He goes out, followed by MARGARET.

JOEL. Hey. Hey, Inspector.

He follows too. The last calls come over the tannoy for destinations all over the country.

During this ROSE *re-enters, still holding her ticket.*

ROSE. Damn.

AAN *comes up to her.*

AAN. Excuse me. Is this Birmingham?

ROSE. No, this is Digbeth Bus Station.

AAN. Very funny.

ROSE. Are you lost?

AAN. No. I'm nervous.

ROSE. Why are you nervous?

AAN. Because this is my first time in England, and . . .

ROSE. Oh, really. Where are you from?

AAN. India.

ROSE. No kidding. You're really from India. I've known loads of Indians and when you ask them where they're from they say Nottingham, Walsall, Leicester. But really India. Great. What's it like?

AAN. It's a lovely country.

ROSE. And you, presumably, grow rice or something?

There is suddenly much noise as the buses rev their engines. The last few latecomers race for their coaches with INSPECTORS *hurrying them along. It is 7 o'clock. Through the haze of diesel fumes, a Polish dance group make a dash for their bus. They sing a stirring chorus of some national song as they board. The coaches move off. The exhaust fumes drift away and the station is more or less deserted.*

AAN, ROSE *and* TOM *are among the very few people remaining.*

The INSPECTOR *passes on the way back from* MARGARET *and* JOEL.

ROSE. Excuse me, has the Liverpool bus come in yet?

INSPECTOR. Come and gone love. Come and gone.

ROSE. Men are such shits!

AAN. I'm sorry.

ROSE. Not you. Not you. Just someone. You don't happen to have . . .

She sees TOM *watching her.*

Oh it doesn't matter.

She crosses to him.

Are you still here then?

TOM. How old are you?

ROSE. Old enough. What about you?

TOM. Do you have anywhere to stay?

ROSE. Oh yes, I'm at the Holiday Inn thank you very much – and yourself?

He gets out his pocket handkerchief and unwraps it. There's a sheaf of notes inside.

ROSE *sits down.*

TOM. Have you still got your ticket?

ROSE. They wouldn't give me the money. If you could just lend me a couple of quid, I'll send it you back . . .

TOM. I'm not totally stupid, you know.

He holds on to a twenty pound note. The rest he puts back in his pocket.

But if you let me take you to a hotel . . .

ROSE. Oh yes? I'm not totally stupid either Uncle John!

TOM. Husband in Saudi Arabia! I want you on that first bus tomorrow morning. Now here . . .

He sorts out some change.

I want you to ring your family. You have family you could ring, yes?

ROSE. Do you?

TOM. Pardon?

ROSE. Let me ask you – what's a man like you doing sitting alone in a bus station at this time of night, offering girls twenty pound notes? You can be arrested for that you know!

TOM. Oh I was not! I am not! Don't think . . . My God . . . I was simply . . . I was expecting to be met myself.

ROSE. And they've not turned up?

TOM. That's right.

ROSE. So why are you worrying about me?

TOM. Because I feel responsible . . . Because I was stupid enough to fall for that silly . . .

AAN has sat down beside them on the bench.

ROSE. And hey has nobody come to meet you? This man comes all the way from India and no one's come to meet him. So you got nothing to moan about.

AAN. I came here to find some friends. Friends of my mother's. But they don't answer my letters so I make a phone call from Victoria and I find they have moved. The people who answered the phone gave me a new address. Walsall.

ROSE (*to* TOM). Now don't you think he speaks good English for someone who's never been to England before?

AAN. I'm a travel agent in India – I've been two days in England. Two nights in London in a bed and breakfast near Victoria, and now this Digbeth Bus Station and I am beginning to form the impression that England is a rather poor country.

TOM. Well – it is.

ROSE. Depends where you go my friend. Depends where you go.

AAN. I am bound for Walsall.

ROSE. Oh.

AAN. And you, sir?

TOM. Oh, uh . . . Castle Bromwich. But I have been left.

ROSE. Give 'em a ring.

TOM. I have. There's no one there except a machine.

ROSE. Is there no one else?

TOM. I do have a friend moved here many years ago.

ROSE. Then give him a ring.

TOM. Her.

ROSE. Oh, her! That sounds more like it. Ring her then. Go on.

TOM. No, it's not that simple . . .

ROSE. Oh, it's like that, is it?

> JOEL *comes in, angry, with his bus ticket.*

JOEL. Damn.

ROSE. Oh dear! Now here's another one!

AAN. Trouble?

JOEL. Ar, you could say that. My bloody bus.

ROSE. You missed it?

> JOEL *throws his bag to the floor and slumps onto the bench.*

JOEL. I mean, I'm going back to my home country. Well, not even going back. The first time. To the country of my family. My racial home. My roots. On account of having had it up to here with this white racist muckheap of a country. Most important thing I ever done. The most important choice I ever made. To get up, pack my bags, go down to Heathrow, get the first plane to Jamaica. And I miss the bloody bus.

AAN. Well, that's a coincidence.

TOM. So we're all let down. Um, I wonder, do you know where Castle Bromwich . . . ?

JOEL. And all because some bloody woman . . .

> *Enter* MARGARET.

MARGARET. Quite impossible.

JOEL. Her. That's her.

MARGARET (*to* AAN). Excuse me please.

> AAN *gets up,* MARGARET *sits in his place.*

TOM. So what's the problem?

MARGARET. Well, the problem is, that I have come here for – well, for a most important meeting . . .

JOEL. No you haven't.

MARGARET. What?

JOEL. You haven't come here for a 'most important meeting'. You've come here to find your daughter. Who presumably ran out on you.

MARGARET. Excuse me. Were you eavesdropping on my conversation?

JOEL. Well, only after you barged into mine.

TOM (*softly*). Now now.

> *Slight pause.*

We have all come here for our own private reasons.

ROSE. Well, speak for yourself.

TOM. All right. Enabled by a generous retirement payment, euphemism for a not particularly generous redundancy, I come here to seek my past. A quest that starts, but I hope doesn't end, with distant relatives in that elusive kingdom Castle Bromwich.

AAN. And so where does it end?

ROSE. He's come to find a woman. It's a lost romance I'll bet. Have I got it right?

TOM. Never you mind.

MARGARET. Right. (*She stands.*) Well, I suppose I had better find myself accommodation. But I assure you in the morning I shall be writing to the Chief Constable and to the Chairman of the Transport Authority. In the strongest possible . . .

> *Enter the* INSPECTOR.

INSPECTOR. All right. Let's have you moving. Time to go.

MARGARET. I beg your pardon?

INSPECTOR. Shutting up time. Not a doss-house. Let's be having you all out.

MARGARET. Inspector . . .

INSPECTOR. Oh, it's you. Well, madam, I have to tell you, this is private property, and if you're not off it in two minutes . . .

ROSE *stands, suddenly.*

ROSE. Well, come on then, Uncle Bobby. Let's be off to our hotel.

MARGARET. Uncle?

TOM. Well in a manner of . . . (*To* INSPECTOR.) Umm, I don't know if you know of any nearby . . . reasonably modest . . .

INSPECTOR. Well, there's the Bon Nuit, round the corner. Cheap and reasonably clean.

TOM. My niece is going off to Belfast in the morning see . . .

ROSE. His niece is of the view, tomorrow is another day.

INSPECTOR. I'll point the way then.

MARGARET. She's pregnant. My God . . .

INSPECTOR. And when I get back, I want you lot absent. (*To* MARGARET.) And that's you in particular.

INSPECTOR *leads* ROSE *and* TOM *out.*

MARGARET. Young man.

JOEL. Yuh, what?

MARGARET. I'm sorry if I barged in. To your talk with the Inspector.

JOEL. Oh. Don't mention it.

MARGARET. I was, you see – I was expecting the police. I'd assumed they'd help me. You see, I've no idea. A teenager, with no money, in a city. No idea at all.

Pause.

JOEL. Yuh, well –

MARGARET. Which is why I wondered if you'd help me.

JOEL. Eh?

MARGARET. Just for the morning. Take me round. Where a runaway teenage girl might go. Or might have gone.

JOEL *looking highly suspiciously at* MARGARET.

You see, she hasn't got any money. So I assume she'll have to go to charities, or doss-houses. And fall into the company of well, I mean, like tramps, and punks, and junkies.

JOEL *still looking blank.*

I mean, presumably you are intimately acquainted with such places and such people.

JOEL. Oh, ar. Yur, sure. Presumably.

MARGARET. Well, then.

She takes out a notebook.

So, then, shall we say, at nine?

JOEL. I'm sorry?

MARGARET. That's too late? Too early?

JOEL (*heavily mocking*). I mean, you know, like nine man, I'n'I tuck up in me bed a snorin and snuffin an stuff like that know what I mean? I mean like, all we rastamen wi we dread an ganga an all we stuff like dat I'n'I gwan rappin and gwan dubbin an hip-hopping an such all de night long, I mean, we no waan fi gi no mout, man, but I mean wey you from?

Pause.

MARGARET. Well, in that case, let's say ten. I noticed, there's a café over there. That's where we'll meet. And plan our strategy.

Pause.

I mean, I'm assuming that you've nothing else on in the morning.

JOEL *looking at his case.*

JOEL. Oh, uh – no.

MARGARET. Well, then, that's settled. And if you prove to be as good a guide as I'm sure you will, then I shall buy you lunch.

JOEL *takes a moment or two to respond to this.*

JOEL (*mock Southern States accent*). Well, thank you, ma'am.

MARGARET. Oh, Margaret, please.

JOEL. Well, thank you, Margaret.

MARGARET (*shutting her notebook*). Don't mention it. So, ten
o'clock, then. Now, I need a hotel. Not, I think, the Bon Nuit.
Um, I don't imagine you know much about . . .

JOEL. The Plough and Harrow? At the Ivy Bush?

MARGARET. Sounds splendid. How do I get there?

JOEL. In a minicab.

> MARGARET *beams at* JOEL.

You got 10p?

MARGARET (*giving* JOEL *10p*). Of course.

> As JOEL *turns to go,* AAN *steps forward.*

AAN. Um, excuse me . . . do you know how I might get to Walsall?

JOEL. No, mate. (*Waving 10p.*) But I know a man who does.

Scene Three

TOM *sits on his bed in the hotel talking to a tape recorder.*

TOM. My diary. If I told the lads they'd never believe me. I'm in a
small hotel with . . . No . . . I found this young girl you see lads
. . . Oh no. This young girl, she just grabbed me . . . No honest,
you can laugh! How did I get into this? This young girl . . .
What could I do? I'll put her on the first bus in the morning.
Oh yes, I will . . . Then I must ring . . . Oh dear . . .

> PATRICIA*'s voice can be heard in the distance.*

PATRICIA. Hallo Tom . . .

TOM. Do you remember me? Oh dear.

Scene Four

ROSE *sits on her bed.*

ROSE. Oh Jesus, Mary and Joseph. Tell him to come. I'll be a good

girl, I promise. Jesus was lost and then was found . . . Holy
Mother, a girl shouldn't be on her own at a time like this, you
tell the sod . . . Oh St Martin, you of the hopeless cases – or is
that the other one? Tell the bastard, I'm sorry, send him back
to me. He did say . . Uncle!

TOM (*calls*). Yes?

ROSE. You got a fag?

Scene Five

The living room of RAVI *and* MISH*'s home.*

RAVI. Remembrance Road.

PUSHBA. No number?

MISH. I don't want you to go. You don't know what kind of
reception you'll get.

PUSHBA. I'll go with you. I'll go up and down the road and knock
on doors and pretend I've lost my way.

RAVI. You don't need to. I'd rather do it myself.

PUSHBA. It'll take too long. Then if Katya comes to the door we'll
know. She won't shout at me.

RAVI. But if he comes to the door – how will we know?

PUSHBA. If he comes – I'll recognise him. It's no use you going,
you won't recognise him.

RAVI. Supposing he's rude?

PUSHBA. He won't be rude. He's not rude.

MISH. I don't think anyone should go. Have you thought what
you're going to say?

PUSHBA. She won't come home.

MISH. I don't want her to come home.

RAVI. I'm not asking her to come home. I just want to know what
the situation is.

Doorbell rings.

PUSHBA. He's here!

RAVI. Right, no more talk about this.

PUSHBA. Why? He could help us find her.

RAVI. No. I don't want the family in India to know about my
daughter. (*To* MISH.) Go, let him in.

PUSHBA. But Mum.

RAVI. Not a word. Do you understand? Tell him nothing.

PUSHBA. OK.

MISH *returns.*

RAVI. Where is he?

MISH. He's paying the taxi driver.

RAVI. It's just typical. Turning up unannounced from India for a
holiday – he might have given us warning – Aan! How nice,
welcome.

PETUE *the cab driver is standing in the room with the bags.*

PETUE. Ah – I'm a taxi driver.

RAVI. Yes your mother said you were in the travel business.

PETUE. No.

AAN. Hallo Ravi.

RAVI. Are you Aan?

AAN. Yes. This is my friend Petue.

PETUE *puts the bags down.*

PETUE. I hope you'll be all right.

AAN. Yes. Yes. They're my friends. This is Mish, yes.

MISH. Hallo Aan.

AAN. And you are?

PUSHBA. I'm Pushba.

AAN. Of course. And Katya?

PUSHBA. She's not here – at the moment.

PETUE. I'll go now. I'll pick you up tomorrow.

AAN. Thank you. Goodnight.

PETUE *exits*.

AAN. He's a very nice man. He drove me around and wouldn't take any money.

RAVI. Really? You're so like your mother.

AAN. I was lost.

RAVI. Well you get the help you need.

MISH. You must be hungry.

RAVI. You must eat. But first, you can wash. Mish you show him his room.

AAN. My mother sent this for you Ravi.

RAVI. Hand painted, silk. Lovely.

AAN. Mish.

MISH. Thank you – you shouldn't have.

> RAVI *is holding the roll of silk against her skirt.*

RAVI. Just right for a wedding.

> AAN *laughs nervously.*
>
> MISH *has opened his present, a pair of embroidered slippers.*

MISH. Thank you. They're wonderful.

AAN. I hope they fit. Pushba this is for you.

PUSHBA. Wow! What are these stones?

> *She is holding up a necklace.*

AAN. Malachite. It's green because it's found near copper.

PUSHBA. Very heavy. Like marble. You must be terribly rich.

MISH. Pushba don't be vulgar.

AAN. This is for Katya – but she's not here so I'll wait if you don't mind and give it to her myself.

MISH. I'll show you to your room now.

> MISH *and* AAN *exit.*

PUSHBA. You're going to have to tell him.

RAVI. If he finds she's living with another man he won't want to marry her. But if we could find her first and get her to come and see him. She might change her mind.

PUSHBA. I don't think that's going to work. She'll smell a rat for a start.

RAVI. I knew it. A holiday indeed. He's come here to marry her.

PUSHBA. Supposing she is married already?

RAVI. That's what we've got to find out.

PUSHBA. Well if she is? I'll marry him.

RAVI. Pushba!

PUSHBA. Funny living in Remembrance Road when you want to forget your family.

RAVI *is looking through the* A to Z.

RAVI. It's not in Birmingham. It's in Coventry. That can't be right.

PUSHBA. He lives in Coventry. That man.

RAVI. How do you know?

PUSHBA. I think she told me once.

RAVI. Is there anything else you know?

PUSHBA. No.

Scene Six

PUSHBA *and* AAN *in the living room.*

PUSHBA. What would you like to do today? I'll be your guide.

AAN. No thanks, I'm meeting Petue.

PUSHBA. Who's he?

AAN. My friend the cab driver.

PUSHBA. Oh that's too bad. I'm free today – all day.

AAN. Have Ravi and Mish gone to work?

PUSHBA. Yes. Ravi said I was to get you lunch.

AAN. I'm not hungry. I want to go and visit Katya.

PUSHBA. I'm not supposed to tell you this but they don't know
where she lives. They have only the name of the road in
Coventry. I know where she lives but I'm not telling anyone.

AAN. What happened?

PUSHBA. She had a row, and ran away one night.

AAN. Is she in trouble?

PUSHBA. I'm not supposed to tell you anything – but they think
she might be married.

AAN. Is she married?

PUSHBA. Nope. But she's in love.

Long pause.

AAN. I'd still like to find her.

PUSHBA. I don't know how you're going to do that.

AAN. But you have her address.

PUSHBA. Well – I did have her address but she's moved. She didn't
trust me. Imagine!

AAN. What does she look like?

PUSHBA (*sighing*). Photos.

She takes a photo album out of her school bag.

Here!

AAN opens the book.

AAN. Is this?

PUSHBA. Katya.

AAN. She's very beautiful.

PUSHBA. Oh that was taken a long time ago. She looks much older
now.

AAN. When was it taken?

PUSHBA. Oh ages ago. Last year. This one's of me.

AAN. It's very nice. Do you have any more?

PUSHBA. Yes, loads. (*Turning the pages.*) This is me on my bicycle.
And this is me with my friends – at the swimming pool. I'm
very photogenic. Everybody says it.

AAN. Are there any more of Katya?

PUSHBA. No. That's the only one. She took all the others with her.

AAN. Can I have this?

PUSHBA. Yes.

AAN. Can I have one of you as well?

PUSHBA. Oh yes. Have as many as you like.

AAN. One will be enough.

PUSHBA. Have the one of me on my bike.

> *Doorbell rings.*

AAN. That will be for me – it's probably Petue.

PUSHBA. My mother thinks Katya might be pregnant. I wasn't supposed to tell you that.

AAN. Why does Ravi think that?

PUSHBA. She was seen going into the maternity hospital by one of our neighbours.

AAN. Pregnant.

> *Doorbell rings again.*

AAN. Look I'll be out all day.

PUSHBA. Are you sure you wouldn't like me to come?

AAN. You're too young for nightclubs. See you later.

> *He exits.*

PUSHBA. Hey! You forgot the photos!

Scene Seven

La Luna Café.

The café MARGARET has chosen is pretty horrible: there is a bar for the purchase of tea and meals; a peanut-dispensing machine; a pin-ball table with a big 'out of order' sign. A knot of people round the bar.

MARGARET is sitting at a table being talked to by ERNEST, who could be any age over thirty.

ERNEST. So I said to them, I'm locked up in here because the devil's put stuff in the water and the only way to stop it is to exorcise the reservoirs. And so I'm tenpence to the shilling. But your government I said your government that pays your wages, finds the eggs have all been poisoned by the capitalists and the only way to stop it is to boil 'em for ten minutes on account that that destroys the poison. And I'm locked up in here on librium and they're up there in Whitehall riding round in Daimlers and telling us to cut down on the fags. You got a light?

MARGARET. Uh, no.

ERNEST. You got a fag?

MARGARET *shakes her head.*

ERNEST. But then, blow me down, if they don't say, Ernest, put like that, you have a point. And I say, all sarcastic like, all right then, if I've got a point, why don't you let me out of here, and let me ride around in Daimlers telling folk to wrap up warm and go easy on the chips. And they says, well, Ernest, we can't do the Daimler, but we will release you, and you can give advice to anyone you want, so long as it ain't us. Ernest, we are returning you to the community.

He gestures around, expansively.

– So here I am. Don't you think it's bloody marvellous?

Enter JOEL, *in a hurry.*

JOEL. Uh . . . Sorry I'm late.

ERNEST. Well, I have enjoyed our chat.

MARGARET. Joel, it is nearly twenty . . .

ERNEST. But if you'll forgive me . . .

JOEL. Ar, I know, I had some trouble . . .

ERNEST. I will go and try and bum a fag off someone else.

ERNEST *goes.*

JOEL. I couldn't find a meter for the motor –

MARGARET. Motor? *Joel.*

JOEL. Consisting as it does of my brother's van which I take out, from time to time.

MARGARET. With his permission.

JOEL. With his blessing. So, I'm sorry I'm so late.

MARGARET. You are forgiven.

JOEL. 'Nother cuppa?

MARGARET. Yes, why not. Anything I'm going to catch, I've caught already.

JOEL. Caught?

NGUGI *comes over.*

NGUGI. Hey, man.

JOEL. Ngugi. How you doing, man?

NGUGI. Hey, Learie. Look who's here. It's Joel.

LEARIE *comes over.*

LEARIE. Hey, Joel. So how you keeping, man?

JOEL. Just fine. Now, this is Mrs Margaret Price.

LEARIE. Well, hi there, Mrs Margaret Price.

MARGARET. How do you do.

JOEL. And perhaps now Mrs P. and I should make a move.

MARGARET. Ah. The voice of action. Well, yes, certainly.

NGUGI *and* LEARIE *look oddly at their friend.*

JOEL. For after all, it's nearly Half Past Ten.

Slight pause.

MARGARET. Indeed.

JOEL. And we have many Nets and Boots and Doss-houses to visit.

Slight pause.

MARGARET. We do.

JOEL. 'Cos if I'm very good, and exploit my intimate knowledge of the demi-monde of Birmingham, and my considerable experience of living on the streets with down-and-outs and tramps and stuff, and we find your deliberately lost daughter in a city of one million people sometime in the next two and a half hours, then I get a Whole Free Lunch.

Slight pause.

MARGARET (*increasingly unsure of* JOEL*'s tone*). Well, yes, that was our, general – strategy.

JOEL (*standing*). So, then, let's Get Ourselves Assembled.

LEARIE. Daughter?

MARGARET. Um, yes.

LEARIE. Lost?

MARGARET. That's right.

LEARIE. And penniless.

MARGARET. Indeed.

NGUGI. Thank the lord you have found us Mrs Price.

MARGARET. Uh, why . . . ?

NGUGI. Because unlike our friend here Joel, whose credentials frankly in this area he has overstated, both Learie and I, in harder times, have some experience of this space. The territory of running off from home and being on the streets and having nowhere like to lay your head, the territory that we gather that your daughter's into?

MARGARET. Yes. (*Pause.*) You see, she's never been, she's never had a day with nothing. Not a day. (*Slight pause.*) And even, with the green hair, and the funny shaved bits, in that, phase, she'd never let it grow out at the roots. Or if she did, she assured us it was all deliberate. (*Pause.*) Which is why I have to find her.

LEARIE. Sure.

NGUGI. Of course. And as a consequence, we would be most delighted to join Joel in his brother's van escorting you in this endeavour.

MARGARET. Uh, you would?

NGUGI. We would indeed.

MARGARET *looks to* JOEL, *who shrugs.*

JOEL. 'A threefold cord is not so quickly broken'.

MARGARET. Joel.

JOEL. Ar?

MARGARET. A word.

They go aside.

JOEL. Yes, Margaret.

MARGARET. Joel. Forgive me. But there is something I have to say. You know, the way you speak. You know, there isn't any need, to put on a special voice, or talk in foreign languages, or quote Shakespeare or whatever, just to impress me. I mean, I'm happy to accept you as you are.

JOEL. I see. Well, thanks.

> *Turning back to* NGUGI *and* LEARIE.

JOEL. So, man, is I'n'I fi lif up an gwine? Or is dem tan in dis place all de day? Cos if dem gwine a find dis gel, am better move deyselves like now, afore the bullman and the babylonians am come a get dem.

LEARIE. Joel . . .

JOEL (*turning to* MARGARET). So, then, you ready like fi mek we tracks, mah? Huh?

MARGARET. I'm sorry?

JOEL. It's not Shakespeare. It's Holy Bible. Ecclesiastes. Chapter Four. Let's go.

MARGARET. Lead me to your brother's van then, Joel.

> JOEL *opens the door for* MARGARET. *She goes out –* JOEL, NGUGI *and* LEARIE *following.*

> ERNEST *attempts to join the party.*

NGUGI. No, Ernest. Not this one.

> *They've gone.*

ERNEST. Pity. A truly fascinating person.

Scene Eight

Hotel Bon Nuit, Reception; and PATRICIA's *flat.*

TOM. Excuse me . . . I have to make a phone call.

RECEPTIONIST. Uncle Bobby is it?

TOM. Who?

RECEPTIONIST. A message for you.

TOM. For me? Oh thank you.

He reads the scrap of paper.

– Oh . . . I thought she was sleeping. When did she, oh dear, where did she, did she say . . . ?

RECEPTIONIST. She said nothing.

She hands him a payphone.

TOM. I see. Oh . . . is this an ordinary phone?

RECEPTIONIST. It's a telephone, you put your money in there . . .

TOM (*doing so*) Ah, I see . . . oh and it tells you how much, very good! Well I never . . . .

He dials. The phone rings in PATRICIA's *flat. There is no one there.*

– And she never said . . . ?

PATRICIA's *voice on the answerphone cuts in*: I am sorry there is no one here to take your call at the moment . . .

TOM *replaces the receiver. He looks for the* RECEPTIONIST.

TOM. Excuse me . . . How do I get my money back? (*The* RECEPTIONIST *has gone.*) Oh dear . . .

Scene Nine

The Net. An advice bureau on accommodation.

A few chairs for people waiting; a low table with leaflets, a counter, notices on the wall.

CLAPPER *and* KAREN – *in their late teens – are at the counter talking to* MISH, *an employee.* KAREN *is pregnant.*

MISH. Clapper.

CLAPPER. That's right.

MISH. Of 23 Acacia Gardens, Nechells.

CLAPPER. Yup.

MISH. So what's the problem?

CLAPPER. Well, this is the problem. Karen.

Enter MARGARET, JOEL, NGUGI *and* LEARIE.

MARGARET. You see, my view, Joel, is the old-fashioned one that one leaves home and sets up on one's own when and only when one has the wherewithal to do so on the basis of one's own resources, without having to rely – uh, this is it?

JOEL *is embarrassed by the fact that* MARGARET *is talking so loudly that* CLAPPER, KAREN *and* MISH *have stopped their conversation.*

JOEL. It is. We sit down here, and wait.

MARGARET. I see.

They sit.

MISH. Go on.

MARGARET (*continues*). Is that man in charge here?

JOEL (*trying to mumble*). Yes.

MARGARET. Extraordinary.

JOEL (*loudly*). What do you mean Margaret?

MARGARET. I think it ought to be a woman, don't you?

MISH. Please go on.

CLAPPER. Karen at present of Flat 1609 John Bright Tower, Aston.

MISH. So?

CLAPPER (*hand on heart, mock dramatic*). And carrying my child.

MISH. I see. And this flat is . . .

KAREN. Well, a friend's. Well, to be honest, an acquaintance. And she won't be – well she won't be either, really, 'less I move out fairly quick. On the grounds of chronic overcrowding.

CLAPPER. Tension.

KAREN. Aggro.

CLAPPER. Bloodshed.

MISH. And Acacia Gardens is a hostel, right?

CLAPPER (*pleased he's got there*). That's right.

MARGARET *attempts to whisper, but she's overheard by*
CLAPPER, MISH *and* KAREN.

MARGARET. So he's in a public hostel.

JOEL. Yes.

MARGARET. And he's got her pregnant.

JOEL. Yuh, that does appear to be the case.

MARGARET. And so presumably he wants the Council to
provide accommodation for him and his mistress and his
child.

MARGARET *has been unaware that* MISH, CLAPPER *and*
KAREN *have turned to listen.*

CLAPPER. Yuh, that's right. What a scrounger.

MISH *hands* CLAPPER *a file.*

MISH. Well, you know the score if you aren't actually
homeless. Here's the list.

CLAPPER *looks disappointed.*

KAREN. Thank you. Come on, Clap.

They go and sit and look at the list. MISH *stands and makes to
go.* MARGARET *and* JOEL *stand.*

MARGARET. I don't think I need to speak to this man. She's
not in an Asian hostel.

JOEL *folds his arms in front of his chest and bars her way out.*

JOEL. Margaret speak to him!

MARGARET. Right – excuse me. What is your name – I like to
know who I'm speaking to.

MISH. Chatterjee.

MARGARET. Is that your first name or your surname?

MISH. Mr Chatterjee.

MARGARET. Could you spell it for me?

MISH. And to whom am I speaking?

MARGARET. My name is Margaret Price. I come from
Oswestry. My daughter's run away from home, and I think
she's in this city, and you apparently house homeless

people, and I'm told it's a good bet that she's been in here.

MISH. And this gentleman is the girl's father?

JOEL. Um –

MARGARET. Certainly not! Here's her photograph. Does it look as if he's her father?

MARGARET shows MISH the photograph. MISH gives it a cursory glance.

MISH. Mrs Price, you understand, we don't provide accommodation for the homeless, here at the Net. We're just an information agency.

MARGARET. Well, it's information that I want.

MISH. I'm afraid that even if I recognised your daughter I wouldn't tell you where she was.

MARGARET. Why not?

MISH. Because I don't know why your daughter ran away from home.

MARGARET. Mr . . . (*Pause.*) What are you implying?

MISH. I'm not implying anything.

MARGARET. Are you a parent Mr . . .

MISH. I am.

MARGARET. And you think you're a better parent than I am?

MISH. I'm not here to contest that.

MARGARET. I resent the fact that you consider yourself more morally responsible a parent than I.

MISH. I don't. I'm simply not going to bend the rules for you.

MARGARET. Extraordinary!

MISH (*handing over the list*). She won't be in a Council home. But unless she's sleeping rough, she might be in one of those.

He stands.

Now if you'll excuse me . . .

MISH exits. MARGARET turns back to JOEL with the list.

MARGARET. Well then. Well, then, at least . . . Do we have an
A to Z?

NGUGI *takes out the list.*

NGUGI. We have the knowledge.

LEARIE. Joel has the knowledge.

NGUGI. Joel has the outer knowledge. You and me, L, got the
inner knowledge.

LEARIE. Right.

KAREN. Excuse me.

MARGARET. Yes?

KAREN. Excuse me, but is the Church of the Assumption hostel on
the list?

MARGARET *takes the list back and looks.*

MARGARET. Uh, yes. It is. D'you know this place?

KAREN. Oh, sure. Half my mates doss there.

MARGARET. And could you – if we took you there, could you
introduce us to your mates? And ask them if they recognise the
picture?

KAREN. Uh . . . Uh, well . . .

She turns to CLAPPER.

CLAPPER. Oh, why not. Help out a maiden in distress. As long as
she's got wheels.

JOEL. Oh, we got wheels.

MARGARET. Indeed. We've *lots* of wheels.

With a slightly jaundiced glance from LEARIE *and* NGUGI *to*
CLAPPER.

– Enough for everyone.

Scene Ten

City centre phone booth and PATRICIA's *flat.* TOM *is in the phone booth.*

PATRICIA *is in her flat, with* TERRY *the Satsuma sales director. The phone rings. She doesn't answer it, but switches on her answerphone to hear who's talking.*

TOM (*amplified on the answerphone*). Hello Pat . . . Tom Llewellyn speaking . . . remember me? Long time no see. I'm in Birmingham see . . . thought it might be nice if we met like. If it's convenient like. It's been a few years I know . . .

PATRICIA (*switching the machine off*). I don't believe it.

TERRY. Who was that?

PATRICIA. When I was a kid back home . . .

TERRY. You're not Welsh?

PATRICIA. Yes.

TERRY. Well I never knew that.

PATRICIA. Why should you?

TERRY. You never said . . .

PATRICIA. Why should I?

TERRY. Well . . .

 PATRICIA *switches the machine on.* TOM *is still speaking.*

TOM (*amplified*). If you could contact me on this number –

 She switches it off again.

TERRY. Why don't you talk to him?

PATRICIA. Why on earth should I? I left home over thirty years ago Terry.

 SUE *is waiting to use the phone.*

 TOM *replaces the receiver.*

 The MUSIC STUDENT *comes by and asks the way.*

JOHAN. Excuse me – The School of Music yes please?

SUE. See the subway? Down the subway, then keep going and there's all building work – mess! When you come to the mess it's either left, right or straight on, OK?

 TOM *comes out of the booth.* SUE *goes in.*

 The STUDENT *departs.*

 PATRICIA *has rewound the tape. They listen.*

TOM'S VOICE. Hello Pat . . . Tom Llewellyn speaking . . .
    remember me?

Scene Eleven

The kitchen of the hostel of the Church of the Assumption. KAREN'*s friends*
MICHELLE *and* SHARON – *both in nighties and dressing gowns – are*
looking at the photograph.

Also in the room are MARGARET, JOEL, CLAPPER, NGUGI, LEARIE
and KAREN *herself.*

MICHELLE. No. No I don't think so. Shar?

    She hands the photograph to SHARON.

SHARON. Uh – don't think so. No.

KAREN. She might have changed her hair.

SHARON. Well, still.

JOEL. Apparently she's well turned out.

SHARON (*handing the photograph back*). But even so.

MARGARET. Well, then. Well, thank you. So, what's the next stop,
    Joel?

    JOEL *looks at his watch.*

JOEL. Well, if you ask me, Mrs P, it's time for your side of the bargain.

MARGARET. You mean, your lunch.

JOEL. That's right.

    SHARON *and* MICHELLE *look at each other.*

MARGARET. Well, I suppose . . . As long as we carry on this
    afternoon.

JOEL. *Of course.*

MARGARET. Well, it's been nice to meet you, um, Michelle and . . .

JOEL. Sharon. Mrs P . . .

    After a moment, MARGARET *decides to bow to the inevitable.*

MARGARET. Unless, that is, you'd like to join us. For a modest
    luncheon.

MICHELLE. Half a minute.

SHARON. Right.

> SHARON *and* MICHELLE *rush out. Pause.* MARGARET *throws a jaundiced glance to* JOEL. KAREN *tries to smooth it over.*

KAREN. She had some trouble with her dad. Michelle. You know, like, over getting drunk, and throwing things about, and getting violent . . .

MARGARET. She's old enough to drink?

JOEL. No, not her. Him.

MARGARET (*to* KAREN). And Sharon?

CLAPPER. Oh, she just didn't like it much at home.

> MARGARET *looks at* CLAPPER, *significantly.*

MARGARET. I see.

> MICHELLE *rushes in, just about dressed, stuffing her shirt into her jeans.*

MICHELLE. OK, then. Ready.

MARGARET. Both of you?

MICHELLE. All three of us.

> *Enter* SHARON *and her friend* DEBBIE, *also assembling themselves.*

> – Uh, this is Sharon's best friend. Debbie.

> *Slight pause.*

DEBBIE. Uh, hallo.

CLAPPER. Inseparable.

Scene Twelve

Street in central Birmingham.

JOHAN, *the Central European* MUSIC STUDENT *is busking. Passers-by pass by.*

Finally, a yuppie couple, HENRY *and* LYNN.

LYNN. Oh, no, of course. You're only on 40 grand a year. We can't afford a *holiday*.

HENRY. Oh, come on, Lynn.

> HENRY *tosses* JOHAN *a coin.*

JOHAN. Thank you.

HENRY. Don't mention it.

JOHAN. Uh, I wonder, do you know the way to . . . uh, the
   School of . . .

HENRY. No, but if I whistle the first few bars I bet you'll pick it up.

> JOHAN *looks blank.* HENRY *laughs and walks on.*

LYNN (*furious*). You bastard.

HENRY. Why?

LYNN. You give him 50p and he's your bloody straight-man.

HENRY. Lynn . . .

Scene Thirteen

The pizzeria.

*In a new covered shopping mall called the Conservatory is a pizzeria called
'Toppings'. The manager is* LUIGI BENNEDOTTI. *On the door are two
security men,* GEORGE JONES *and* TED WILSON. *There is a screened
but not boothed telephone.*

*We become aware of an altercation at the doorway to the restaurant. Leaving
his colleague* GEORGE *in charge,* TED WILSON *comes up to* LUIGI
BENNEDOTTI; *as* SAMANTHA *and* ESTELLE – *lunching out as a
treat – give their order to the waitress* TRACY.

SAMANTHA. So I'd like a Jumpin' Jumbo but with mozzarella
   instead of mushrooms and a slice of spicy sausage, please. Oh, ·
   some artichoke. And perhaps some extra pepperoni.

TRACY. Uh, I think that's actually a Sergeant Pepper.

ESTELLE. And I'd like the diet special. Which appears to be
   essentially a pizza without pizza.

TRACY. There in one.

> TED WILSON *has reached* LUIGI.

TED. Uh, sir. Uh, Mr Bennedotti.

LUIGI. Ted. What can I do for you?

TED. It's at the door. It's, uh, a party.

LUIGI. So, there's a problem?

TED. Well, sir. There is a number problem. And a dress-code problem. And I'd suspect a decibel level problem. And potentially, I'd say a payment problem.

LUIGI. Then no entry. Then no problem.

TED. Well, that's what I thought. And what I said. But they wouldn't go.

LUIGI. Then call the police. No problem.

TED. Well, that was my thought too, sir, but . . .

MARGARET *bursts into the restaurant past* GEORGE.

GEORGE. Eh, madam. Eh, eh, you.

MARGARET *collars* TRACY.

MARGARET. Where is the manager? Is there somebody in charge of this establishment?

TRACY. Uh, it's Mr Bennedotti . . . Would you like a table, ma'am –

TED. The problem.

LUIGI. Yes, I see. Now, madam. I'm the manager. Can I assist you?

MARGARET. Yes, you can. I have a party outside whom I planned to take to lunch in this establishment. But which has been denied admittance, by what I can only call a Storm-trooper you've posted at the door. On grounds that, variously, it goes against company policy, it's more than his job's worth and if he lets us do it they'll all want to.

Slight pause.

LUIGI. Um . . .

MARGARET. And while I was all for writing a sharp letter to the local newspaper, my chief associate preferred to organise what amounts to a blockade. Of which I cannot say I approve, but am not empowered to prevent. So there it is. Mr Bonnedutti.

LUIGI. Bennedotti. Mr Wilson, we will temporarily waive what adds up to rules two to seven.

TED. You mean . . .

LUIGI. Yes. Let them in.

> TED, *a little disconsolate, goes off to tell* GEORGE *to let in the party.*

MARGARET. Thank you.

> LUIGI *has a second thought.*

LUIGI. That is, assuming, madam, that you can meet the bill?

> MARGARET *opens her bag, to find her purse, and opens that.*

MARGARET. Well, Mr Bennedotti, if you like, you're at liberty to telephone my banker.

> *She notices something odd in her purse but shuts it delicately.*

But I had hoped that my word would be sufficient.

LUIGI (*who has seen the group enter*). Yes. Yes, I'm sure.

> *The group now consists of* JOEL, NGUGI *and* LEARIE *from La Luna;* CLAPPER *and* KAREN *from the Net;* DEBBIE, MICHELLE *and* SHARON *from the hostel and three new faces:* TRISHA, AHMED *and* BONES.

> LUIGI *and* TRACY *attend to the party.*

> MARGARET *comes over and joins them, and everything is assembled.*

CLAPPER. Well, thank you my man.

KAREN. So, where's our table?

DEBBIE. I wanna be by the window.

SHARON. I don't. I feel sick.

MICHELLE. That's 'cos you came up in the glass lift.

TRISHA. Ooh I love those lifts.

LUIGI. So, madam, is this satisfactory?

AHMED. It is perfect.

BONES. It's ideal.

MARGARET. Yes, it'll do.

> TRACY *hands out menus.*

TRACY. The pasta special's cannelloni, the special topping is asparagus and spicy sausage and the soup is vegetable noodle.

But we're out of noodles. So it's only vegetable.

CLAPPER. I demand a refund.

TRACY. You've not paid nothing yet.

CLAPPER. Give this girl a Nobel Prize.

MARGARET (*to* LUIGI). Um, do you have a telephone?

LUIGI. Yes, of course, ma'am.

He guides her over to the telephone and leaves as MARGARET *dials.*

TRACY. Right now, is everyone ready to order?

Everybody babbles together.

JOEL. Hey Ngugi. Show some leadership.

NGUGI. You show some leadership.

JOEL *nods to indicate he has something else to do.*

All right, now. Quiet everybody. Everybody quiet. Now I shall read out the selections and you put your hands up when we hit the one you fancy. Number one – the Dolce Vita.

Two hands go up and the table freezes.

We 'cut' to MARGARET *who is talking on the phone and is being overheard by* JOEL.

MARGARET. Hello, Norman?

Yes, of course it's me.

Well, Norman, I'm in Birmingham. I'm looking for our daughter.

Well, to be quite honest, because if I'd told you I don't think you'd have been that pleased. And it seems that I'd be right.

We cut back to the table, where the freeze breaks.

NGUGI. The Onassis. Tuna, feta cheese, greek olive.

No hands go up.

TRACY. And tomato.

One hand goes up.

NGUGI. Any advance on one for the Onassis.

Table freezes and cut to MARGARET *and* JOEL.

MARGARET. Well, Norman, I hardly think that's my fault. As soon as you started shrieking at each other I went straight off to the kitchen. As you know full well, I hate rows.

All right, yes. I hate rows that I didn't start. In other words I'm human, Norman.

Back to the table.

NGUGI. The Marinara? The Four Seasons? Peeping Tom?

AHMED *and* DEBBIE *hands up.*

AHMED. With extra mozzarella.

NGUGI. That's two for Peeping Tom, one with extra cheese.

DEBBIE. Hey, why can't I have extra cheese?

NGUGI. Correction, two with extra cheese.

Freeze and cut back to MARGARET *and* JOEL.

MARGARET. – Well, that's why I rang you, Norman. Yes, I found out this minute. Literally, when I opened up my purse.

No, I shan't tell the police.

Well, obviously.

Well, Norman, it's not as if we know that much about her genes. This is the very problem. Now I have to go.

She puts the phone down, turns, and finds JOEL *there.*

MARGARET. Joel.

JOEL. All right, Margaret.

NGUGI. Right, I make that nine. So we're one short. (*He looks round.*) Own up, own up.

TRISHA. Where are you, errant orderer?

CLAPPER *slowly raises his hand, to general groans.*

Freeze and cut back to MARGARET *and* JOEL.

JOEL. All right, yes, I was eavesdropping. And it was very wicked of me. But it did prove quite instructive.

MARGARET. What do you mean?

JOEL. Well, I mean in terms of (a) your husband didn't know you'd come to Birmingham; (b) that there does appear to be a reason Sandra ran away, viz her starting shrieking and you slipping off into the kitchen; (c) that she's nicked your, what? your money? bank card? and (d) if I read the word 'genes' right that Sandra may not be exactly what you might call in all senses yours. Do I get this roughly right?

MARGARET. How dare you.

JOEL. Dunno. Do I get an answer?

Cut back to table.

CLAPPER. No I thought I wouldn't have a pizza. On account of its grossisity. No, I thought I'd go for cream-cheese stuffed spinach tortellini served al dente dusted with a grating of fresh parmesan adorned with home-made basil and tomato sauce enhanced with a mixed salad of the season graced with thousand island blue cheese creamy garlic or house dressing on the side.

KAREN. Oh, Clapper.

CLAPPER. Or maybe I'll have a Peeping Tom instead.

Freeze and cut back.

MARGARET. All right. Not that it's any of your business. But Sandra is indeed adopted. After her mother died in childbirth. As we told her at the age of ten. And indeed she had an argument, a fairly forthright argument with my husband, shortly before she left, though I've no reason to suppose . . . And, (b) or (c), in fact, it does appear she's got my Access card. All right? Is that honest enough for you?

JOEL. Yes. I'm sorry.

MARGARET. What about?

JOEL. Well, your Access card.

MARGARET. Well I must say it's pretty low, in my present scale of worries.

JOEL. 'Cos of course it makes our job a nightmare.

MARGARET. Why?

JOEL. Because if she got access, as it were, to Access . . . Then she could be staying, shopping, bopping anywhere.

MARGARET. I see. Yes, yes of course.

JOEL *turns back to the table.*

MARGARET. Uh, Joel . . .

JOEL. Mm?

MARGARET. When you say 'our job'?

JOEL. Well. Being a lumpen unemployable. Me gotta kep meself
outta mischief somehows, in'I?

> *He turns quickly to avoid* MARGARET'*s reaction, and goes back to
> the table, followed by* MARGARET.

NGUGI. . . . three coke floats, a sasparilla special, two banana
milkshakes, four green salads and a diet 7-up with ice, and that
is it.

JOEL. Plus for me a marinara and a coke, and for our hostess . . .

MARGARET. Oh, um –

JOEL (*taking the menu from* TRACY). You're not a veggie are you?

MARGARET. I am absolutely not a vegetarian.

JOEL (*handing it back*). Miss Piggy.

TRACY. Small or large?

JOEL. A jumbo.

> MARGARET *decides to react with quiet dignity. She and* JOEL *sit, as*
> TRACY *withdraws.*

JOEL. Right, team. Like, we have a new conundrum to address.
Instead of a homeless down and out, we have a lateish teenager
into hip-hop who comes here from a sheltered if not repressed
background.

MARGARET. Joel . . .

JOEL. And like everybody, wants a good time of an evening in the
city. But unlike everybody, she has if not unlimited then
considerable access to riches beyond the dreams of avarice.
She has on the basis of one easily forged signature her little
fingers stuck into a tub of gold.

MICHELLE. Phew.

> *The young people look at each other.*

LEARIE. She's into black music.

JOEL. Yuh.

BONES. But she isn't black.

JOEL. A moment's thought, Bones.

KAREN. And is she – like, does she do drugs?

MARGARET. She certainly does not.

JOEL. Don't know.

   Pause.

DEBBIE. Well, I'd say – Fifth Avenue. The Glitterati.

TRISHA. Trash. Or Crumpets. Or the Weir.

SHARON. The Bubblebath.

MICHELLE. Or if not . . .

KAREN. Then, De Loreans.

Scene Fourteen

The bus station. Crowds of people coming and going.

We focus on the queue for tickets. A conversation has developed between some
PENSIONERS *in the queue.* TOM LLEWELLYN *is amongst them.*

REG. I mean it's as I say, you've only got one life . . .

TOM. If you don't do it now, you'll never do it!

VI. The world's a very small place nowadays.

TOM. It is, it is. And there's some wonderful places in the world .. .

GWEN. Matlock Bath.

TOM. I'm sorry.

GWEN. That's a wonderful place.

VI. Matlock Bath?

GWEN. Oh yes! You can go up in a lift there.

TOM. Is that a fact?

GWEN. Just like the Alps, it is.

VI. Anyway, we said – let's do it!

REG. You see, when you're at work you don't realise!

TOM. That's right! That's right!

REG. I've got up at six o'clock every morning for the last fifty years.

GWEN. My old man never gets up.

TOM. You don't realise, do you – there's a whole world going on out there!

REG. That's right! We was mugs! I never missed a day!

TOM. Nor me . . .

VI. So when he retired I took him up town. He couldn't believe it!

REG. Why aren't all these buggers at work? I said. Every bloody day the town is packed!

VI. He still can't get over it.

REG. I can't. We went in the travel agent . . .

VI. He couldn't believe it.

REG. There is no place in the world you cannot go! I said to Vi – Vi, life's too short!

TOM. Everyone in our street's been to Spain you know?

VI. They've been all over in our street.

GWEN. Have they been to Matlock Bath?

TOM. I know a couple has been to Hawaii. And they thought nothing of it!

VI. Didn't they? It looks lovely on the telly.

REG. We've got the brochure.

VI. Oh we've got all the brochures. You can't see our coffee table!

REG. Bahamas . . .

VI. Bali Hi – you know – where *South Pacific* comes from.

They reach the front of the queue.

REG. Two to Blackpool please.

TOM. Well I said when I got my redundancy – this is it now; I've done my work, I've paid my dues, I'm going to bloody enjoy myself! There's a whole bloody world out there!

GWEN. Go to Matlock Bath!

TOM. I will, I will. I'm a free man you see . . .

> TOM *hears a familiar voice.*

ROSE. Excuse me . . . Has the Liverpool bus come in yet?

> TOM *and* ROSE *spot each other.*

REG (*going*). All the best then mate!

TOM. Thank you.

VI. Tarra.

> *They go.*

GWEN (*to the* TICKET CLERK). Matlock Bath please . . . tomorrow morning.

> *The* CLERK *recognises her.*

Hello! Yes, it's me again. How are you? Is your dad better?

> ROSE *comes over to* TOM.

ROSE. So you really are a dirty old man who hangs round bus stations!

TOM. I'm going back home.

ROSE. Oh no!

TOM. And why aren't you? You promised me!

ROSE. Did you not find your woman then?

GWEN. Tarra then . . .

> *She goes.*

TOM. Bye . . . (*Steps out of the queue.*) Carry on . . . .

ROSE. Could you not find her?

TOM. It doesn't matter. I think I've waited long enough.

ROSE. Have you not even seen her?

TOM. I left a message. It was an answerphone.

ROSE. Another one? Does no one in your family talk to one another no more?

TOM. Looks like that doesn't it? I left a number for her to call me back. I waited but she never called. They're good I suppose

answerphones. Save a lot of embarrassment really. She
obviously doesn't want to talk.

ROSE. How do you know? She's probably away!

TOM. Oh she was. She was in Brussels yesterday, she's in London
today. She's at the Computer Exhibition all next week. She has
a phone in her car, she appears to live alone . . . oh I know all
about her – she left a message on the machine you see – oh I
know all about her, I know exactly where she is. She's even left
a number where she could be contacted.

ROSE. Did you ring it?

TOM. No, no.

ROSE. Why ever not?

TOM. That's only for if it's urgent.

ROSE. You come all this way and it's not urgent? Not urgent . . .

TOM. I'm going home. It was a bad idea. Stupid . . .

ROSE. God, you don't half give up easy!

TOM. Do I? You don't do you?

ROSE. Me?

TOM. Still waiting for the Liverpool bus to come in?

ROSE. No I am not! Sod him! Listen Frank . . .

TOM. Tom.

ROSE. You get yourself along to that Exhibition. I bet you she'll be
thrilled to see you!

TOM. You think?

ROSE. Of course she will! And thanks for that night in the hotel by
the way – I slept like a baby!

TOM. Then in the morning you'd gone . . . You promised me you'd
go home!

ROSE. And you gave me that money, I know. But isn't that just the
luckiest thing that I didn't go? Because I bet you don't know
where the Exhibition place is now, do you?

TOM. No I haven't a clue.

ROSE. Well I do, and I'll tell you what we'll do Uncle. I bet you're hungry aren't you? Why don't you buy us both a nice cup of coffee and then I'll show you the way to the Exhibition. She will be so thrilled to see you!

TOM. No.

ROSE. Tom, you've not even spoken to the woman, how do you know? You know nothing! That's men all over – think they know it all when they know nothing! Now come on . . . I know where it is . . .

TOM. It's not till next Wednesday. I'm going home.

ROSE. No you're not! Now come on now! You done me a favour, I'll do you a favour – I tell you what we'll do. You stay the weekend and I'll take you places you've never been and show you sights the like of which you've never seen! Then come Wednesday morning, you and I we'll go to the Exhibition and there will be this woman . . . what's her name?

TOM. Pat.

ROSE. Who's never got married because she's been waiting for you all these years . . . Imagine that? Can you imagine – and you're about to go home!

SOLDIER. Are you in this queue mate?

TOM *has to make a decision.*

TOM. No . . . no, it's all right. (*To* ROSE.) So what are these wonderful sights then?

Scene Fifteen

The Canopy.

It's Wild West night at the Canopy Discotheque. The DJ *ascends from below stage in a lift into the central space. He is wearing a stetson and he fires off two sharp shooters.*

DJ. Howdy all you dirtscratchers, cowhands, pigstealers, hired hands, and all you gals. Howdy. Allow me to introduce myself, Wild Blue O'Driscoll is the name and tonight this here disco is coming from the Wild West at the Canopy, brought to you by Bronco Beer. Stick around partners for the Clint Eastwood Lookalike Contest, and a fashion parade from Hot Sox of

Moseley. Now slug it out! This here's a party.

'OK Sam – pick that banjo to pieces!'

After this we see AAN *and* PETUE *arrive.*

PETUE. I don't see why you wanted to come here. We've had cream tea at Stratford-upon-Avon, burgers at Dudley Zoo. We've been to Aston Hall, Villa Park, the famous Queensway underpass, Macaroni Junction.

AAN. I wanted to find a beach.

PETUE. Why don't we go to the Nights of the Raj and get something to eat. A friend of mine works there.

AAN. I wanted to find out what the English are like at home.

Long pause as they take in the Wild West Disco.

Is this typical?

Enter TRACY *and her lad* GARY – *she as a vestal virgin, he in a toga.*

TRACY. Wild West. Wild West. And I told you, double check the brochure. Ancient Rome's next week.

GARY. I said I'm sorry. Wanna drink?

TRACY. I'll have a Southern Comfort.

A CENTURION *crosses in front.*

GARY. Well, at least we're not the only ones.

Enter JOEL *and* MARGARET.

JOEL. Well, Mrs P. The Canopy. So what d'ya think?

MARGARET. This is a nightmare.

JOEL. Hey, come on, man. Dis joint is jumpin'.

MARGARET. Joel, please don't call me man.

JOEL. De lights is flashin' and de sounds is hot.

MARGARET. I mean, we have been this evening to the Crumpets. Rubbish.

JOEL. Trash.

MARGART. The Waterbed.

JOEL. Not bad. In fact, the Bubblebath.

MARGARET. That place they wouldn't let you in . . .

JOEL. Those places that they wouldn't let you in . . .

MARGARET. And I still do not believe that there is not a place in Birmingham on Saturday where it is possible for nice young people both to dance and talk. But, here we are. You have the photos?

JOEL. Uh, well, actually . . .

MARGARET. Yes, what?

JOEL. Well, Mrs P, I wondered if we might give it a rest now. Have a dance, enjoy ourselves.

MARGARET. Joel, as I have always said, indeed as I have told you, if a job's worth starting, it's worth finishing.

Pause. JOEL, *wearily, takes out two photographs.*

JOEL. I'll do the floor. You do upstairs.

MARGARET. Right.

JOEL. And I'll meet you in Annie Oakley's Old Saloon in half an hour.

MARGARET. Uh, what?

JOEL. The bar.

Two young women approach a bar, WENDY *and* KELLY. *They are both hairdressers, dressed as southern belles.*

They are examining the cocktail list.

There is a large sign for Bronco Beer behind the bar.

WENDY. A Gringo Gunsling? A Prickly Cactus? I don't recognise anything. What's a Coyote Bite?

KELLY. I think a Prickly Cactus is tequila.

WENDY (*to the* BARMAN). Two Tomahawks please!

KELLY is eyeing the talent. WENDY *pays for the drinks.*

DJ. Howdy partners! Do I hear it?

ALL. Howdy!

DJ. Time to draw up yer wagon. Clear a space for Hot Sox all the way from Moseley, with the latest trail blazers for all you cowgals and pals. Squaws and braves get ready. And all those lovely Southern Belles that everybody'd like to tinkle.

Immediate entrance of Hot Sox mannequins, male and female.

After a while the attention is focused on TOM *and* ROSE *outside the club.*

TOM. So where do you stay?

ROSE. I've told you, I have this friend, I doss on her floor, but the night is yet young . . .

TOM. You might be young . . .

ROSE. Come on.

TOM. No, no, I liked the Four Green Fields. I liked the Shamrock – loud but very good. The Ceilidh on the Canal Boat – very unusual. Now I think I've had it, I really do think . . .

ROSE. Oh shut up your moaning.

They go in.

TOM. My God, what is this place?

ROSE. I bet you've never seen nothing like this in Llanelli?

They go to the bar.

The focus shifts to AAN *and* PETUE.

PETUE. I came to this country with great respect. Do you know many English?

AAN. I met some English people on holiday last year. They gave me their address.

PETUE. I always had respect – but since I've been here I've lost that respect. Now if I see an Englishman in my country – I wouldn't help him. I wouldn't want to know. This is a racist country. I am not welcome here.

A large black Indian Chief with war paint and full headdress passes.

– My parents have paid £35,000 in fees in the five years I've been here studying Business Administration. I was wanting to go to work here after my graduation – I needed to go back to the Punjab with work experience. I have an MA – but you see I am a cab driver. So I am going home next month.

AAN. You say it's racist. But give me a specific example,

PETUE. I went for a job interview with a firm of accountants. At the end of the interview they said they had no vacancy for me because they were an English firm. 'English' that was the word they used. I got up – and as I was leaving the room I heard a noise behind me, before they closed the door. I didn't look back because the noise made me afraid. It was the sound of laughter.

AAN. But I think perhaps there aren't even jobs for the English anymore.

PETUE. But the laughter? Can you explain that?

Another Indian, this time an ordinary BRAVE *comes up.*

BRAVE. Do you have a light?

PETUE *takes out his lighter. The* BRAVE *lights a long peace pipe.*

BRAVE. Thanks.

He goes.

DJ. After this the moment you've all been waiting for – 'Go ahead punk, make my day!'

Elsewhere at the bar MARGARET *is being talked at by* ERNEST.

ERNEST. No, look, you talk about London having everything, but I see it another way. True, London's got a one-way, but we got a one-way, and London's got a Post Office tower, but we got a Post Office tower. But has London got a Rotunda? Answer me that.

JOEL *appears.*

It is very noisy so this scene is shouted.

JOEL. So, any luck?

MARGARET. I beg your pardon . . .

JOEL. Any luck?

MARGARET.No, you?

JOEL. No. Do you want a drink? A Paleface or a Dry Possum?

MARGARET. I'll have a small sherry.

JOEL. Medium or sweet?

DJ. No 1: Steve from Walsall. 'Don't insult my mule.'

The first contestant has made a studied entrance: he is followed by the second.

DJ. No 2: Dave from Redditch. 'So long old man!'

Several other Clint Eastwood Lookalikes appear, but the act doesn't get very far before ROSE *begins to heckle.*

ROSE. Get him off! Boring. Boring!

TOM. Come on. I think we should go.

ROSE. Oh, leave me alone.

TOM. You're drunk!

ROSE. And you're a boring old fart! Now piss off!

TOM. Listen, you must look after yourself.

ROSE. Oh really Mr Boring Old Fart and why is that?

TOM. You're pregnant and shouldn't be here.

ROSE. Is that a fact?

TOM. Boozing and smoking and dancing!

ROSE. And why not?

TOM. You're too bloody young for a start and you're pregnant! You have to start to do things different. Have you booked into a doctor's even? A clinic?

ROSE. And why should I do that?

TOM. So they can keep an eye on you!

ROSE. Why? Why? I don't want no one keeping an eye on me thank you very much! That's all people ever do is keep an eye on you! I suppose you're keeping an eye on me! Why is everyone always keeping an eye on me! Well you can all sod off! It's my baby. It's not your baby. I bet you couldn't even have a baby if you tried!

TOM. Rose, it's not only your baby! When the father turns up . . .

ROSE. What father? There is no father!

TOM. In Liverpool.

ROSE. Who says he's the father? How do you know he's the father? He might not be the father. And he's not coming! Do you understand that – he's not coming! He's not coming. This child has no father!

She goes off.

TOM. Rose!

> *The platform occupied by the* DJ *is descending.*

DJ. Everybody feeling funky! Yeah?

ALL. Yeah!

DJ. OK. You sure are pretty enough for a skunk. OK! Hit it!

> *The* DJ *has disappeared.*

> JOEL *is dancing.* MARGARET *taps his shoulder and he leaves the floor and goes with her.*

MARGARET. Joel, I'm going.

JOEL. Hey, Margaret. You can't go. It's just beginning to hot up.

MARGARET. Yes, that's what I'm afraid of. Shall we meet tomorrow?

JOEL. You'll miss the Can Can competition. Not to mention the Bronco Body Poppers. There's a Knife Act.

MARGARET. Call me in the morning, Joel.

JOEL. 'K.

> *She turns to go.*

JOEL. Hey, Margaret.

> *She turns back.*

JOEL. Sweet dreams.

MARGARET. I'll try.

> *Focus shifts to* PETUE *and* AAN.

PETUE. I've been here five years and I have no girlfriend. Because you see I don't go to pubs or discos. How can I? I don't drink. This may surprise you.

AAN. But what about your family? Surely they can introduce you to girls.

PETUE. They are all in the Punjab.

Focus shifts to TOM *and* ROSE.

TOM *finds* ROSE *crying.*

TOM. Rose . . .

ROSE. Please help me, Uncle Bobby . . . Please help me! Don't
leave me, I have no one. No one in the world but you . . .

Focus shifts back to AAN *and* PETUE.

PETUE. Look! Look over there. An Asian woman and a white man
dancing – that's what becomes of them.

AAN gets to his feet in a daze.

AAN. Katya. It's Katya.

PETUE *watches him in wonder.* AAN *suddenly seizes* KATYA *by the
arm and tries to drag her away from her partner.*

PETUE. Don't.

PETUE *leaps to his feet to protect* AAN *from the inevitable.* MARTIN,
the man dancing with KATYA, *grabs* AAN *by his jacket.*

KATYA (*screams*). No!

MARTIN. Let go of her; she's with me.

AAN. She's not. She's coming with me.

KATYA. Please go away.

AAN. It's me. Aan.

KATYA. I know. Pushba told me. It doesn't make any difference. Go
away.

The Club BOUNCERS *arrive and bundle all of them towards the
door.* KATYA *vanishes in the crowds.*

BOUNCERS. OK, OK. Break it up.

MARTIN *shoves one of the* BOUNCERS *away from him.*

MARTIN. Get your hands off me.

Fighting breaks out.

Then there is sudden silence and TOM *with* ROSE, MARGARET
and AAN *appear in isolated spots at the front of the stage.*

TOM. Late night in Birmingham. The sound of sirens. Ask me, it's
the Wild West every night. And an old man from a valley trying

to remember what he's here for, looking for a woman who he hasn't seen for thirty years and the one thing that he knows is she won't be the same.

MARGARET. Late night in Birmingham. The smell of what I take to be some class of frying chicken. Meeting people, going places, that I never thought existed. And perhaps I wish I had.

AAN. Late night in Birmingham. The policemen missed me in the dark. The hot metallic smell of blood and sweat. And having found her, I lost her again.

End of Act One

ACT TWO

Scene One

A dance routine for pregnant women led by KATYA. *The women are lying on their backs, moving their legs to the rhythm of the music, rather like the Follies.*

KATYA. One ... Two ... Three ... Four ...

> *At the end of the dance routine everybody gets up.*

> Now find a space on the floor. Enough to turn around in with your arms outstretched.

> *She demonstrates.*

TOM. Aren't you glad I brought you?

> TOM *is sitting along the wall watching* ROSE. CLAPPER *is watching* KAREN.

> AAN *enters and sits by* TOM *and* CLAPPER.

KATYA. Face me ... Take a deep breath and pretend that you have a lift inside ... draw the lift up from your pelvis to the top of your rib-cage ... hold it there ... now let the lift gently down again. And again, breathe in, let the lift up ... and hold it ... now down again ...

> Good.

> *Turning her attention to* TOM *and* AAN.

> Excuse me please, you men join in. You can help your wives at the birth by doing the exercises now.

AAN. Katya!

KATYA. What are you doing here?

AAN. Pushba.

KATYA. No excuses. Fathers must join in.

TOM. But I'm not the father.

MELDIA. That's what they all say, love!

General laughter.

TOM. No but really. She – I – brought her here so that she could learn to breathe.

AAN. Katya!

KATYA. Look you either join in or wait outside.

TOM. And I've got this bad back see . . .

    KATYA *gives up on* TOM. *Turning to* CLAPPER.

KATYA. And you?

CLAPPER. Same here.

KAREN. Clapper, if you don't get down here now it gets called Beverley.

CLAPPER. But what if –

KAREN. Either way.

    CLAPPER *bows to the inevitable, as does* AAN, *both joining the women.*

KATYA. Now everybody lie down. I want you to circle your feet out – eight times. And then in eight times.

    She walks between the bodies on the floor.

    Anyone here who's not doing this for the first time?

MAY. Me.

MELDIA. And me.

KATYA. How was it last time?

MAY. This will be my second baby. I came to classes because I've honestly forgotten how to do it. It was so long ago. Five years.

KATYA. What about you?

MELDIA. It'll be my fourth.

KATYA. My goodness. I hope you're getting plenty of sleep.

MELDIA. I go to bed with the children.

KATYA. That's very good.

ROSE (*to* TOM). Four, blimey. She looks young.

TOM. Well that's encouraging isn't it.

KATYA. All right. Now I want you to concentrate on your toes. Tighten them. And relax. Good. Tighten and relax. Can you still see your toes Mrs White?

MRS WHITE. Just about.

MELDIA. I can't.

KATYA. Who paints your toe nails?

MELDIA. My husband.

KATYA. Isn't he good to you. Now ankles. Tighten and relax.

MAY. I want lots of flowers when I have my baby, I'm looking forward to that – a whole room full of them.

KATYA. Knees.

WINSOME (*a black girl*). I'm worried. They say when you have a baby you fight a lot with your man. I'm really worried about the fights.

KATYA. Bottoms.

MELDIA. Do you fight now?

WINSOME. No. Hardly at all.

KATYA. Tummy.

MELDIA. Well then. You won't fight. Babies bring people closer together.

KATYA. Shoulders. Tighten and relax please! This is a very good way to relax even when you're not pregnant.

MAY. What really gets me – is you go to all that trouble and then some idiot says: 'He looks the spitting image of his daddy'! That really annoys me. I hope I have a girl this time.

KATYA. Eyes.

ROSE. How can you tighten your eyes. This isn't relaxation, this is torture!

KATYA. All right now. Go back to the first exercise. The lift from your pelvis to the top of the rib-cage again.

They all straighten up.

TOM. What's the matter Rose?

ROSE. They all have husbands. This is making me awful lonely.

MRS WHITE. I started painting the kitchen. And then the bathroom looked bad – the walls were dirty so I painted the bathroom. And all that was because I started to get the room ready for the baby.

WINSOME. I know. Once you start decorating you can't stop. We're moving house.

ROSE (*to* TOM). You see. They've all got homes, and houses and things.

ROSE makes a move to go.

TOM. Where are you going?

ROSE. Out of here. It's depressing me.

She exits, followed by TOM.

KATYA. Is she all right?

TOM. It's all right. I'll take care of it.

KATYA. Take a break now everyone. There's coffee on the table. The health visitor will be talking to you about breast feeding in ten minutes.

The women cross to the table. AAN *remains with* KATYA.

KATYA. What are you doing here?

AAN. I came to apologise for my behaviour. Why have you left home?

KATYA. That doesn't sound like an apology.

AAN. Ravi's very worried about you.

KATYA. My mother sent you?

AAN. She didn't send me: she doesn't know where you are.

KATYA. OK. So now you've apologised.

AAN. You haven't answered my question.

KATYA. It's none of your business.

AAN. Yes I know – but we were friends once.

KATYA. That was a long time ago, we were kids.

AAN. Could we go somewhere. I had pictured a beach.

KATYA. You're so simple, aren't you. Life is so simple for you.

RITA BRACEBRIDGE, *a woman in her mid to late thirties, the health visitor, arrives.*

RITA. Hi Kathy!

KATYA. Hallo Rita.

RITA. Is this your young man?

KATYA. No. This is Aan.

AAN. Hallo.

They shake hands.

RITA. Nice to meet you.

KATYA. He's here on holiday from India.

RITA. India, really? You're not from Nottingham or Leicester?

AAN (*fed up*). I'm really Indian.

RITA. How are they today? Any problems?

KATYA. May looks tired.

RITA. OK Kathy. I'll have a word with her.

RITA *crosses to the table.*

AAN. Kathy? That's not your name.

KATYA. What's the point, they call me Kathy anyway.

AAN. What does he call you?

KATYA. Doesn't call me anything. Never uses my name.

AAN. Why?

KATYA. That's not true. If he calls my name I tremble.

AAN. Katya.

KATYA. Love. He calls me love.

AAN. He's asking a lot. He's asking you to give up your family for him.

KATYA. He's not. They have given me up.

AAN. Have they met him?

KATYA. Only Pushba. My father refuses – and my mother can't without offending my father.

AAN. I came too late to find you.

KATYA. Wait here. I've got to make a phone call, then we can go.

> AAN *waits. The* WOMEN *return.*

RITA. Today we're going to talk about why breast is best.

> Just sit yourselves down there wherever you can. Take the weight off. Now breast feeding even if you can only manage the first few weeks is essential to bonding.

WINSOME. To what – bondage?

MELDIA. Bonding.

WINSOME. Oh.

RITA. You can take notes if you like – you look very tired May.

MAY. Me? I'm still working.

RITA. Tut. Tut. Tut. Right. Engorged breasts, flat nipples, sore nipples, cracked nipples and blocked ducts. Just some of the topics I'll cover today. And here's a booklet you might find useful, *How to Survive the First Week of Breast Feeding.*

> Now the thing to remember is that a baby's sucking mechanism is so strong and so instinctive that if you put a baby to a seventy-year-old grandmother's nipple it will draw milk. So you see anyone can breast feed.

MAY.
MELDIA.
WINSOME.   } (*triumphantly addressing* AAN). Men can't!
MRS WHITE.

Scene Two

The park.

MARGARET *enters looking at a piece of paper. A shout from off-stage.*

JULIE. Wayne! Wayne, you come back here!

> WAYNE *roller-skates on to the stage and falls.*

WAYNE. Ow!

> *Enter* WAYNE'*s mother* JULIE, *with baby buggy and* LEE *in tow.*

LEE. Eh Mum. Can I 'ave an ice-cream?

JULIE. No, you can't. Oh, Wayne.

LEE. Oh, come on, Mum.

JULIE. Your trousers. Look at you. *No*, Lee.

> WAYNE *clambering to his feet.*

MARGARET. Excuse me.

JULIE. Ar?

MARGARET. I'm looking for amusements.

JULIE. What?

LEE. Aw, go on, Mum.

MARGARET. You know, the slides and swings and things.

LEE. Eh, Mum.

JULIE. Oh, Jesus Christ.

LEE. Eh, are we going to the amusements? Oh, are we, Mum?

JULIE. No, Lee. We're not going to the amusements. I've gorra get
you to your nan's so I can get to work.

> WAYNE *has roller-skated off.*

LEE. Aw, *Mum.*

> JULIE *drags* LEE *and the buggy off after* WAYNE.

JULIE. Wayne! Just you come back here!

> *They are gone.*

> MARGARET *breathes deeply.*

MARGARET. Oh Lord in Heaven.

> HENRY *and* LYNN, *the yuppie couple, walk by. They are talking.*

HENRY. So I said, what on earth do people *do* in Telford, and he
said that he wouldn't shift for less than 50K, a turbo and a
carphone –

LYNN. Not six weeks in the summer? But I do understand, a
carphone . . .

MARGARET. Um, excuse me . . .

> *But they're gone.* MARGARET *shrugs and turns to go herself. She sees*

something alarming, turns back, and hides. Enter NGUGI, LEARIE, DEBBIE, MICHELLE, SHARON, TRISHA, ASHMED *and* BONES.

NGUGI. Right, comrades. It is a simple choice that faces us. The lake, caff, sculpture garden or amusements.

MICHELLE. Oh, 'musements, 'musements.

AHMED. Caff.

SHARON. We just had tea.

TRISHA. We know that. You was sick.

SHARON. Just once.

DEBBIE. I wanna feed the ducks.

BONES. I wanna kill the ducks.

MICHELLE. Oh, Bones.

NGUGI. I'd say – the lake.

MOST PEOPLE (*variously*). Oh, no . . .

LEARIE. And the amusements after.

As they go:

SHARON. I bet you anything I'm sick . . .

And when they're gone MARGARET *goes out another way.*

Scene Three

At the playground.

Children playing on swings, etc, watched by their parents. JOEL *sits on a bench, much of which is taken up by a sleeping tramp, partially covered in newspaper and using his bundle of possessions as a pillow.* JULIE, LEE *and the baby and* WAYNE *enter.* WAYNE *is carrying his roller-skates.*

JULIE. All right. You can have a play. Ten minutes. As long as you leave those bloody skates alone.

WAYNE *goes towards the swings.*

LEE. I wanna swing.

JULIE. Of course you want a bloody swing.

> JULIE *takes the baby and* LEE *away to give* LEE *a swing as* MARGARET *enters.*

MARGARET. Joel, I'm sorry.

JOEL. Well, Mrs P.

MARGARET. I couldn't find the way.

> JOEL *is sending up* MARGARET'*s style.*

JOEL. Well, Mrs P, if you just left those extra minutes . . .

MARGARET. May I sit down?

> JOEL *stands.* MARGARET *looks at the tramp.*

> Thank you.

> *She sits.*

> I'm sorry, there's not room . . .

JOEL. It doesn't matter. I've been sitting down all morning. (*Slight pause.*) Now, Council of War.

MARGARET. Well, yes.

JOEL. You don't sound enthusiastic.

MARGARET. Well, I'm not.

JOEL (*sending her up again*). Well, you know, Joel, I was always taught, if a job's worth starting then it's worth . . .

MARGARET. Oh, shut up Joel.

> *Slight pause.*

> I apologise.

> *Pause.*

> It's just – you're right. It's a city of a million people. And I think we could go into discos, boutiques and Kentucky Fried whatevers until kingdom come, and I don't think anyone would recognise her.

> *She's very upset, almost crying.* JOEL *wants to comfort her, but it's awkward that he's standing and she's sitting.*

> *Suddenly angry.*

> Oh, I do wish that that man would *get up*.

But all the tramp does is groan a little, MARGARET *stands quickly.*

What right does he have to take up a whole bench. It's just – typical.

JOEL. Uh, what of, Margaret?

MARGARET. This city. This whole place. Look at that family. I saw them earlier. She's going out to work. She's leaving those children with their grandmother, no doubt because father's run off with another woman . . . Doubtless leaving us to pay the bills . . .

JOEL. When you say us . . . ?

MARGARET. Well, I mean, Joel, people who pay rates and taxes. So that people can have children and not look after them. And I know that it's not a fashionable opinion, but my view is, as a man sows, so shall he reap. And I know you, in your community, Joel, I know your people have a different attitude to things like marriage, and well, work, and that's all fine, but if you expect the taxpayer . . .

JOEL. Now that is it.

MARGARET. What's what?

JOEL. That is the last straw, Mrs P. I'm off.

MARGARET. And that's another thing. You start a job, and you can't finish it.

JOEL. Shut up.

MARGARET. No gumption. No commitment. No . . . I beg your pardon?

JOEL. Granted. But before I'm off. I have to tell you why. Which is because I've had it up to here. I have listened to your views and your opinions, or rather, I have listened to your prejudices and your stereotypes. I have been lectured and I've been told off for the way I live and your bizarre view of how what you insist on calling 'my community' behaves. And all the time, I'm doing you a favour. And while I'm sorry Norman didn't come up trumps or babies, and I'm sure it isn't all your fault with Sandra, and for your sake I still hope you find her, there's a little bit of me, well actually a quite big bit, that thinks that for her sake it might be better if you didn't. There's a Next we haven't tried in Harborne and a Benetton's in Acocks Green. Oh, and a winebar called 'Old Smokey'. Good luck, Mrs P.

He turns as if to go. But he doesn't really want to.

Meanwhile, JULIE, LEE *and the baby return to* WAYNE.

JULIE. Now Wayne, we gotta go.

WAYNE. Aw Mum. I wanna do the fireman's pole.

JULIE. Oh, Wayne. D'you have to.

LEE. And I wanna slide.

The baby starts crying. WAYNE *rushes off.*

As JULIE *looks to her baby,* LEE *climbs up the slide.*

JULIE. Oh, Barry.

MARGARET. Joel.

Pause.

JOEL (*not turning*). Yes Mrs P.

MARGARET. Joel, there is something I should tell you.

JOEL. Tell away.

MARGARET. Not here.

JOEL. Not here, not me.

Pause.

MARGARET *moves to* JOEL *and away from the others.*

MARGARET. It wasn't Norman, Joel.

Slight pause.

JOEL. What d'you mean?

MARGARET. It wasn't his fault, that we couldn't have a baby of our own.

JOEL. Now, Mrs P, I have to tell you, modern medical opinion is more or less unanimous . . .

MARGARET. Because of my – my termination. Of my own.

Pause.

JOEL. You what?

MARGARET. You see, then, when I was 17, you couldn't get it legally. And they often botched it. And he was, the father was a trumpet player. With a stupid, no hope jazz band. So we had to find the cheapest. And the cheapest that you went, the more, more likely you'd be botched.

Pause. JOEL *doesn't know what to say.*

– Well, as you say, there's another Next and a few more winebars. I'll leave you to – have a damn good crow.

She rushes out.

JOEL *can't work out which is uppermost – pity for* MARGARET *or anger at her last remark. He throws himself back on the bench beside the tramp.*

JOEL. Oh, Margaret.

JULIE. Oh, Barry, what's the bloody matter?

JOEL *is alerted to movement beside him. The tramp sits up. It's* ERNEST.

ERNEST. Well, if it isn't Neptune, Lord of all the Vasty Deep.

JOEL. Well, hello Ernest.

ERNEST. You know, they say it's chlorine makes it all go green, but I know better. It's the channel tunnel.

JOEL. Sorry?

ERNEST. They've got to make the water green so we won't notice when they pipe the water from the sea. Because the reservoirs are all in Welsh. I spotted it when they blew the gaffe and called it Channel Four.

JOEL. You what?

ERNEST. But if you really want to find her, then I'd ask around the hairdressers.

JOEL. Yuh, sure. Thanks, Ernest.

He gets up, then.

Say that again.

ERNEST. Well, it stands to reason. You don't recognise a person comes in buys a skirt, or a piece of chicken.

JOEL. You were listening.

ERNEST. But somebody whose hair you're cutting. Well, you get to know 'em. As a I recall from my own haircut days.

JOEL. You used to be a barber?

ERNEST. No. I used to have my hair cut.

JOEL. Ernest, you're a bloody genius.

> *He calls off-stage.*

> Hey, Margaret!

ERNEST. Recognition no less welcome for being somewhat overdue.

JOEL. Hey, Margaret!

> MARGARET *re-enters.*

MARGARET. Joel, I'm sorry. That was most unfair.

JOEL. Margaret, I've got it. Or rather Ernest's got it.

MARGARET. Ernest?

ERNEST. Good morning.

JOEL. It's her roots. It's Sandra's roots.

MARGARET. Joel, is this a rather tasteless reference . . .

JOEL. Her hair. And how she wouldn't let the roots go. And so she will almost certainly have had it done. And paid, of course, by Access.

> *Pause.*

MARGARET. How many hairdressers are there in Birmingham?

JOEL. I've no idea. We'll have to find a Yell . . .

> ERNEST *has found a tattered Yellow Pages in his bundle.*

ERNEST. Ahem.

MARGARET. Well, look at that.

> *She goes and sits with the Yellow Pages.*

> What a wonderful coincidence.

ERNEST. I find it useful for the – well, the more fundamental needs of life.

MARGARET. Uh, yes.

> *She lets the book lie in her lap.*

JOEL (*taking the book*). Oh, give it here. Guest Houses, Haberdashers . . Hairdressers.

MARGARET. Well.

JOEL. Well, there's a lot. Three pages.

MARGARET. Then we better make a start.

To ERNEST.

Um, I wonder, Mr Ernest, if we might, well, borrow . ... .

ERNEST. I insist you have it.

MARGARET (*feeling in her purse*). Obviously, you'll let me buy you . . .

She hands ERNEST *a coin.*

ERNEST. Thank you ever so.

MARGARET. Now, Joel, just before we go, I should say that I'm very . . .

She is interrupted by a terrible wail from JULIE, *at* LEE, *who is at the top of the slide ladder, but not on the slide.*

JULIE. Oh, bloody hell. Oh, Lee. Oh, what's the matter now?

LEE. Mum. I don' wanna.

JULIE. Well come down then.

LEE. No I can't.

JULIE. Oh, Jesus Christ, Lee.

MARGARET. Oh, for heaven's sake.

MARGARET *goes to the slide, gives her bag and* ERNEST*'s newspaper to* JULIE.

MARGARET. Excuse me, would you hold that please?

MARGARET *climbs up the ladder, picks up* LEE, *puts him on the slide and pushes.* LEE *slides down the slide.* MARGARET *is about to climb down the ladder, when she makes a decision. She gets on the slide.*

JOEL. Bloody hell. Hey, Margaret, should you . . .

LEE *is shocked by events, but not too shocked to get off the bottom of the slide.* MARGARET *slides down the slide. She gets up, brushes herself down. She takes the bag, but not the paper, from* JULIE.

MARGARET. Thank you. Well, that's much better. Shall we go?

She strides out, followed by a bemused JOEL.

ERNEST (*to the equally bemused* JULIE). One should never underestimate the usefulness of strangers. Can I have my paper, please?

As ERNEST, JULIE *and family go out,* RITA *crosses the stage in wellingtons, with a gardening basket, looking on. She exits.*

AAN *and* KATYA *enter. They sit on a bank, throwing bread to the ducks.*

KATYA. It's a big city, isn't it?

AAN. I don't know if I could live in a place like this all the time. I think I'd miss the sound of the sea and the fishing villages, and the fruit trees. Although I like city nights and the clubs, I'd also miss our weather.

KATYA. Monsoons?

AAN. I like lightning and watching the day go to night. I'd miss that, it's very grey here, isn't it?

KATYA. You get used to it.

AAN. Do you remember when you came to visit us?

KATYA. I do. It was the best holiday – we haven't been away since. My abiding memory is cows crossing the road without any warning. You'd only just passed your driving test: 'Would you like a beef-steak?', you'd say. I was terrified.

AAN *takes a small package out of his shoulder bag.*

AAN. I've brought you something.

KATYA *opens it, a very delicate mobile of tinkling white shells in the shape of hearts.*

KATYA. It's beautiful.

AAN. They're made at a fishing village near my home. They come from the Beach of Shells.

KATYA. I remember. I've still got the photographs. Pushba was with us.

AAN. I don't remember that.

KATYA. You collected hundreds of shells for her. And when we got back they stank out the house – and Ravi threw them all away. Poor Pushba cried for days.

AAN. That's funny. I don't remember her being with us.

KATYA. I remember something else too. Five years ago when I went to India I wanted to be lost in a sea of brown faces. I really didn't want to stand out. But I found they didn't want me to. They wouldn't let me lose myself that way. I stood out there just as much as I do here. And everybody thought we were rich because we came from England. I knew then there was no perfect place – where I could be happy. That I would find it with someone.

AAN. I know. That I understand too.

KATYA. The person isn't always the obvious one, and the place isn't ever perfect.

Pause.

Why haven't you ever married?

AAN. I don't know. I will sometime. My mother hopes I've come to marry you.

KATYA. Why have you come?

AAN. A holiday.

KATYA. Is that all?

AAN. I might study here.

KATYA. Study what?

AAN. Business. My father would pay.

KATYA. Don't. Please don't. This is a hard country if you haven't grown up in it.

AAN. I don't understand. You don't want me to come?

KATYA. You are so perfectly dignified in your own country. You would lose it here.

AAN. What would I lose?

KATYA. Your dignity.

AAN. But you've just said there's no perfect place.

KATYA. Life's more complex than happiness you know.

AAN. Then I must be very simple-minded indeed.

KATYA. Don't misunderstand me. I'm glad you've come. I'm sure now I've made the right decision.

AAN. And there's no possibility you will change your mind?

KATYA. I'm not going back: since I was a teenager my mother has considered nothing else but who I might marry. Consequently she's introduced me to about fifteen potential husbands. And I'm getting a little tired of it.

AAN. Fifteen! No wonder you left.

KATYA. Come and meet him – will you, for my sake.

She gets up to leave. He joins her.

AAN. Yes. I'll meet him.

KATYA (*going off*). Ring me.

AAN. What's your English man's name?

KATYA. Murphy. (*Calling as she leaves*). Martin Murphy.

Scene Four

The Manager and Manageresses of three hairdressing salons appear under separate lights.

ELAINE. Hallo, 'Cut and Run', Elaine speaking. Yes.

CARLA. Hi there. 'Le Snip'. Please hold.

DAVID. Hallo, That's right, it's 'Topcrop' and I'm David.

ELAINE. I'm sorry, but you'll have to, it's a dreadful . . .

CARLA. Hallo, it's Carla, sorry to have kept you, what can I . . .

DAVID. Well, yes, it would depend of course what method . . .

ELAINE. Oh, dear. I'm sorry. But it's quite against our policy.

CARLA. No well I've looked, no record of a Mary, sorry, of a Margaret Price.

DAVID. No, well, in fact you see, we don't keep records, that is, other than our regulars. So we can't help you. Bye.

Scene Five

The Exhibition Centre. The Computer Show is on.

A glimpse of the future, with something of a fairground atmosphere. The software and hardware companies with names like Kiwi, Mango, Lycheescript and the Fruit Machine, all have stalls with smart women doing sales presentations.

There are crowds of people. There is music and above it all, the voices of the women all speaking at once:

FRANCESCA. – What we know is that it is going to be increasingly hard to survive in this business unless you have some kind of graphics computing facility and that is the great advantage of the Grapefruit . . . .

SUKIE. No one will survive in this business without some kind of graphics computing ability and the great advantage of the Tangerine is that it turns your P.C. into a powerful presentation graphics workstation . . .

MANDIP. The great advantage of the Kiwi is that it turns your P.C. into a powerful presentation graphics workstation and we believe that in the Clementine, we are approaching the ultimate artists tool . . .

LULU. We believe in the Imaginator we have the ultimate artists' tool and now with PP3 it is within your grasp. With simple menu operation, eight pen turret, liquid ball and fibre tip – what could be more flexible?

The attention is then directed towards the Satsuma stand. Jugglers and magicians perform in front of a curtain.

CELESTINE. Ladies and gentlemen, welcome to the Satsuma Experience!

ROSE is pursuing BRENDAN – a catering assistant, as he pushes his trolley through the crowd.

ROSE. Is it good money here then?

BRENDAN. Terrible, but better than the hotel.

ROSE. Any jobs going?

BRENDAN. Are you not working at the hotel now?

ROSE. Have you ever seen a pregnant waitress? They kicked me out

– and out of my room. I'm homeless . . .

TOM. Here you are! I thought I'd lost you!

BRENDAN. I'll have to get on Rose, I'm being watched. I'll see you.

ROSE. Tonight?

BRENDAN. Sound – come up Caesar's.

He goes.

ROSE (*to* TOM). Have you found her?

TOM. Who was that?

ROSE. A friend.

TOM. What's his name?

ROSE. I can't remember.

TOM. Have you known him long?

ROSE. No. I don't know him really.

TOM. But you're meeting him tonight?

ROSE. Yes, yes, I might. What's the matter. Are you jealous or something?

TOM. No, no . . .

ROSE. You are! Oh Uncle, you're jealous! Don't worry, I still love you! I tell you something Uncle, my mother, God rest her soul, married the only man she ever kissed. That's not for me – I will have all the lovers I choose.

TOM. You must be careful these days . . .

ROSE. That's right – you get engaged to them, you soon find out what they're like – this one here . . . (*Points to a ring on her finger.*) All sweetness and light he was. We got engaged and he thought he owned me! This one . . . (*Points to another ring.*) thought it was a licence to kill. Broke my bloody nose! This one . . . agh – I thought I knew this one.

You're right, you've got to be careful!

TOM. Right.

ROSE. But not too careful or you end up like you – 65 and still looking for your first love!

TOM. Fifty–five!

ROSE. And where is she?

TOM. I don't know, they all look the same . . .

MAGICIAN. Could you pick a card please.

TOM. What's this?

ROSE. It's a con, to get you on the stand.

MAGICIAN. Now would all those with hearts step forward please.

TOM. I have!

> *The curtains start to open revealing a woman demonstrating the systems. GWEN is passing by. She stops to watch.*

ROSE. Of course you have! Everyone has – it's a trick Dumbo – to get you on the stand. Come on!

TOM. Wait! It's her . . .

ROSE. Where?

TOM. There! That's her . . .

> *They start to move forward.*

PATRICIA. We at Satsuma recognise that the aim of every business must be to increase productivity at a technical level and thereby increase profitability. To achieve this we have produced for our customers, the ultimate workstation.

The Satsuma segment SE1 includes window presentation manager with SE4 multi-tasking graphical user environment. The Satsuma philosophy being to recognise . . . (*She spots* TOM.) to recognise . . . to recognise the need for a new breed and we believe we have the ideal vehicle in the, in this, in the Satsuma, in the workstation. So, in a few moments, my colleague will now demonstrate the dynamic data exchange and, and . . . thank you.

> *She goes out through a small door.*

TOM. My word!

ROSE. She recognised you! She recognised you!

TOM. She did?

ROSE. Didn't you notice? Come on!

> *As they go round the back, one of the crowd speaks to GWEN.*

GEORGE. Interesting isn't it?

GWEN. Have you ever been to Matlock Bath?

> JOHAN *comes on playing his fiddle.*

> *Meanwhile, in the tiny back room on the stand.* PATRICIA *sits, head in hands.* TERRY *is raging.*

TERRY. What happened? What's the matter with you? The Satsuma segment SEXX and XX3 with pips as well as window presentation – did you even mention it? Optional multiserver and internet support – did I hear that? I don't think so!

PATRICIA. It's not the end of the world. I was only talking to a few old fogies who wanted to rest their feet.

TERRY. You don't know who you were talking to! You never know! They might own a bank for all you know. You cannot go on appearances!

> ROSE *looks in.*

ROSE. Excuse me . . .

TERRY. Not in here! It says private, can't you read?

PATRICIA. What do you want? Come in . . .

TERRY. Patricia!

PATRICIA. But Terry – she might own a bank.

TERRY. Five minutes you've got – then it's Network Security and it had better be good!

> TERRY *goes.* ROSE *has come in followed by* TOM. PATRICIA *stares at him.*

TOM. Hallo . . .

PATRICIA. Tom Llewellyn . . .

ROSE. That's right! He's come all the way from Wales just to see you

PATRICIA. You've what?

ROSE. And we liked your talk out there. Very good!

TOM. Oh yes. Did you understand it?

PATRICIA. Me? I wrote it. Did you?

TOM. Not a word.

PATRICIA. Well I was thrown so . . . Listen I have very little time . . .

TOM. Right, we mustn't hold you up.

ROSE. Sit down! Isn't he terrible? I'm sure she's got a minute.

PATRICIA. Tom Llewellyn . . . You've not really come all this way, not simply to see me, have you? No . . .

TOM. There's very few things . . . There's a few moments in your life, looking back, a few things you value, a few question marks and you've only got one life. I thought, while I still can . . .

So . . .

PATRICIA. So . . .

TOM. You look like you're doing all right anyway. Are you?

PATRICIA. Doing all right? Oh yes thank you boyo! Well I was. I achieved 150% of my target this month. I get fêted for that. I will have dinners given in my honour. Harpists will play. I shall get to go on the President's trip. It was Rio last year. This year I believe it's Bangkok.

TOM. Bloody hell! I never imagined . . .

PATRICIA. Oh it beats teaching, I can tell you. Mind you if I slip to 90% of my target then I'm out and my name will never be spoken of again. So it's tough . . .

TOM. But worth it?

PATRICIA. It's the future Tom, with ot without me and I intend to make damn sure that it's with me! It's all right – I'm lucky, I don't need sleep and I have no family, so as long as I don't do another presentation like that last one . . .

TOM. We distracted you, I'm sorry. We'll go . . .

PATRICIA. No, it wasn't your fault. I'm having a roller coaster of a week and then you turn up – my mind flipped.

TOM. I'm sorry. Look we'll go.

PATRICIA. OK, but it is nice to see you.

ROSE. Now wait a minute!

PATRICIA. I'm sorry?

ROSE. This man has come half way across this land to see you!

TOM. It's all right Rose. It was just nice to make contact, that's all . . .

ROSE. That's all! That's all! What's the matter with you both! Come
on now – make an arrangement – give her a big smacking kiss
– do something! Have you not seen the films! This is your big
moment, come on! Jesus, men are useless! Oww!

TOM. Rose . . .

ROSE. Don't mind me! Just get on with it! Oww!

PATRICIA (*referring to* ROSE). And who's this?

ROSE. I'm nobody, but this is your man. This is your long lost
. . .Oww!

TOM. This is Rose.

ROSE (*in pain*). Uncle!

PATRICIA. Your niece?

ROSE. Oh yes, I'm very niece. Could you get me to a hospital?

TOM. Rose! You're not . . . ? Oh God! She's pregnant, see.

PATRICIA. I can see that! Well she can't have it here!

TOM. Lie down Rose!

ROSE. No fear! It was those damn classes! I told you they was no
good for you – all that swinging your legs in the air. If that's
natural then I'm a monkey's . . . Oww!

TOM. The doctor said lie down! She's a special case.

ROSE. And so's he, honest! All the way from Wales he's come.

A head looks in.

CELESTINE. Pat . . .

PATRICIA. Not now Celestine! Not now!

CELESTINE *goes.*

ROSE. Ow!

TOM. There's a bed at the hospital. We must . . .

PATRICIA. Celestine!

TOM. She's only seven months . . .

PATRICIA. Oh my God!

CELESTINE *comes back.*

Celestine could you speak for ten minutes on Network Security?

CELESTINE. I don't know.

PATRICIA. Well now's your chance to find out.

CELESTINE. Will Terry mind?

PATRICIA. Yes. But so will his wife if I tell her how long he spends at my flat, so I think he'll understand. Come on.

TOM. Are you sure?

ROSE. Of course she's sure! She's dying to get out of here. She wants to talk to you Uncle!

She sits on a chair.

Now one of you grab the legs and the other take the back. That's the idea. Now off we go. Oww!

So you didn't expect this, did you now? Are you surprised?

PATRICIA *is speechless. They carry her off, possibly through the crowds of spectators and jugglers, etc.*

End of scene. As ROSE *is carried off and we return to the main hall,* CELESTINE *is revealed beginning her presentation.* REG *and* VI *are her audience.*

CELESTINE. Good afternoon ladies and gentlemen . . . My name is Celestine and I want to talk to you about how your floppy drive access can be restricted . . .

REG. Excuse me!

CELESTINE. Yes?

REG. Have you got any free brochures?

Scene Six

Godiva's hair salon.

First, in a spot of light, we see PAM, *the Manageress of Godiva's, on the phone:*

PAM. Good afternoon. Godiva's. Pam.

Pause.

Well I suppose . . . Why not?

Pause.

Hold on.

Full lights. There are three areas: the desk, staffed by PAM, where customers wait to be taken to be costumed; the colour and wash area, where SAMANTHA colours, KELLY manicures and ESTELLE beautifies (in this sequence, she is waxing legs, which she does in a curtained area); and the styling area where WENDY cuts hair.

At present, JULIE is waiting to be coloured by SAMANTHA; KELLY is just finishing painting RAVI's fingernails; the heavily pregnant WINSOME – whom we remember from the hospital – is in the next chair, waiting for her fingernails to dry; and LYNN is waiting to be styled by WENDY.

WENDY calls from off:

WENDY. Ro! Ro!

RO, a harrassed trainee, rushes across the stage with a large, full basin.

RO. I'm coming!

ESTELLE enters and crosses towards the screened area with MRS DYSART.

ESTELLE. Right now, Mrs Dysart, will it be half, full leg or bikini line today?

MRS DYSART. Oh, the full works, please, Estelle.

ESTELLE. Full works. In November. Well, Mrs Dysart, mine is not to reason why.

She pulls the curtains round MRS DYSART. KELLY checks WINSOME's fingernails.

KELLY. Right then, Winsome. Ro!

RO rushes back in, now carrying the top half of a drier.

RO. Uh – yuh?

KELLY. Wash Winsome and then hand her on to Wendy, there's a love.

KELLY goes out. RO doesn't know where to take WINSOME.

RO (*to* KELLY'*s back*). Uh, where do I . . . (*To explain herself to* WINSOME:) I'm sorry, I'm the ET, see.

WINSOME. No one need ever know.

She leads the grateful RO *out.*

SAMANTHA *and* JULIE.

JULIE. Bikini line?

SAMANTHA. Leg waxing. D'you want one?

JULIE. Oh. No thanks.

SAMANTHA. The same again?

JULIE. Well, no, if you don't mind.

SAMANTHA. How could I? Though I thought it was lovely.

JULIE. So did I.

KELLY *leaves as* PUSHBA *arrives.*

PUSHBA. Ah, Mummy, there you are. I've been looking everywhere.

RAVI. Pushba. You've news? Of Katya?

PUSHBA. Yeah. But before I say anything, you must please remember I am just the messenger.

RAVI. What do you mean?

PUSHBA. I mean it's not my fault.

Transfer focus to WENDY'*s chair.* LYNN *is settling herself into the chair for* WENDY *to cut it.*

WENDY. Right, then. As per?

LYNN. That's right.

WENDY. That dovetail, did it work out?

LYNN. Fine.

Pause as WENDY *begins.*

WENDY. So are you going to a party then? Or something special?

LYNN. No. No, nothing special. Really.

Transfer focus to main desk. MARGARET *and* JOEL *arrive.*

PAM. Hallo.

MARGARET. Um – is it Pam?

PAM. That's right.

MARGARET. I'm Mrs Price. I telephoned.

Transfer back to colourists' room.

SAMANTHA. So you think he'd like it beechwood?

JULIE. Well, he'd *like* it bright red. But there's limits.

SAMANTHA. Too right there is. We'll do a half head henna, and if he doesn't go for it, then more fool him, say I.

SAMANTHA *starts to work on* JULIE.

RAVI. So did he tell you this?

PUSHBA. He didn't need to. He came back looking like a man who's been turned down.

RAVI. Where *is* she?

PUSHBA. That I couldn't tell you.

KELLY *returns.* RAVI *has let her hands drop, endangering the manicure.*

KELLY. Now, *Mrs C.*

RAVI *raises her hands again.*

RAVI. I'm sorry.

KELLY. I should think so.

KELLY *is busying herself with equipment.*

PUSHBA. There's more.

RAVI. Go on. It couldn't be worse.

PUSHBA. Yes it could. She wants to be married.

KELLY *decides to absent herself. She heads off to* SAMANTHA *and* JULIE.

RAVI. What?

PUSHBA. To Martin Murphy. He's a doctor at the hospital.

KELLY *comes up to* JULIE.

KELLY. Now, do we want a manicure today?

She takes one of JULIE*'s hands.*

Ooh. Tt. Sort out those half moons.

JULIE. Uh . . . Uh, no . Not this time. Thanks all the same.

SAMANTHA *and* KELLY *look at each other.*

RAVI (*upset*). Well, I don't care. As long as she doesn't think she'll get my blessing.

PUSHBA. Well, that's the point. Do you want to hear Plan B?

Transfer to WENDY *and* LYNN.

WENDY. So are you going to get away for Christmas?

LYNN. No. No, I don't think so.

WENDY. Ah. (*Pause.*) A lot of mine go skiing now. Not sure I fancy it. Do you?

LYNN. No, not a lot.

WENDY. Well then. But I suppose . . .

PAM *and* MARGARET *arrive;* JOEL *has been left at the reception area.*

PAM. Wendy, can I have a word?

WENDY. 'Scuse I.

WENDY *leaves* LYNN *and goes to* PAM *and* MARGARET.

Transfer to RAVI, PUSHBA, KELLY, SAMANTHA *and* JULIE.

RAVI. So you think that if I gave my blessing she'd change her mind and not marry this Martin Murphy after all.

PUSHBA. I'm convinced of it.

RAVI. How very strange.

PUSHBA. Yes, isn't it. Do you want to hear Plan A?

Back to WENDY *and* LYNN.

PAM *and* MARGARET *have moved on.*

WENDY. Well. Missing woman. Had her hair done here last week. On my day off.

LYNN *doesn't respond.*

Oh, I'm sorry. You were saying.

LYNN *says nothing.*

Skiing. You were saying why you didn't fancy skiing.

LYNN. No I wasn't. *You* were.

She turns to the slightly thrown WENDY.

But you're right I don't much fancy it. And even if I did I probably wouldn't get the chance. Because unlike the rest of your fascinating clientele I don't go on interesting holidays. I don't have an interesting time. I'm a boring housewife. And the one thing that I really like is getting shot of house and wifery and going out and doing things alone.

She turns back. Pause.

WENDY. OK.

Shift focus to PUSHBA, RAVI, SAMANTHA, KELLY *and* JULIE.

RAVI. I don't believe you. You mean to say this man hasn't even *asked* her yet?

PUSHBA. That's right. But Englishmen are so slow. Anyway – the point is – why should he ask her, when her family refuse to recognise him. You see the dilemma. Which is why you must recognise him, give them your blessing, welcome him into the family. Then he'll propose to her and she'll say no.

That's it. Plan B can't work without Plan A.

RAVI. So, is he living with her?

PUSHBA. Yes.

RAVI. Oh, no.

PAM and MARGARET *arrive.*

PAM. Well, hallo there Mrs Chatterjee. It's nice to meet your daughter.

PUSHBA. Pushba. And I'm off.

RAVI. Pushba!

PUSHBA. You see, she's happy, and she loves him, Mummy. That's the problem. Bye!

PUSHBA scuttles out. RAVI *makes to rise.* KELLY *is quickly there.*

KELLY. Now, don't you dare.

PAM. What a lovely girl. You must be proud.

RAVI. Oh, yes.

> PAM *and* MARGARET *go to* SAMANTHA, *as* KELLY *looks at* RAVI*'s nails.*

Oh, definitely.

> *Focus shifts to* WENDY *and* LYNN. RO *is bringing* WINSOME *in to sit and wait for her haircut.*

RO. Uh, Winsome.

WENDY. Winsome? Oh, Winsome. Hi there Winsome. Won't be long.

WINSOME. Hi there, Wendy. Thank you Ro.

RO. Uh, Ro? Oh, me. No trouble.

> RO *smiles, turns, trips, recovers and exits.*

WINSOME. Apparently, ET.

> *A moment before* WENDY *gets it.*

WENDY. Oh, yes.

(*To* LYNN:) So, what d'you do before?

> *Slight pause.*

LYNN. Before?

WENDY. You married.

> *Focus shifts to* SAMANTHA, PAM, JULIE, MARGARET *and* KELLY, *returning from* RAVI.

> SAMANTHA *is looking at the photo.*

SAMANTHA. Yes. I remember. Thursday. And she had a friend. She was brought by one of Estelle's regulars. You know, the *nie danke* badges and dungarees. Estelle!

MARGARET. The dungarees?

> *Focus shifts to* WENDY *and* LYNN.

WENDY. So what d'you lecture in?

> *Slight pause.*

LYNN. Art History. My specialism was the Post-Impressionists.

WENDY. The Post-Impressionists.

LYNN. That's right.

Slight pause.

WENDY. You mean like Seurat, Bonnard. Gauguin. Vuillard. Stuff like that.

LYNN *turns to* WENDY.

LYNN. That's right.

Focus shifts to SAMANTHA, KELLY, MARGARET, PAM. JULIE, *joined by* ESTELLE.

ESTELLE. Oh, you mean Ms Bracebridge. My Ms Bracebridge from the hospital. I'm her one indulgence. She says that everyone should have one. And I'm it.

PAM. And she writes cheques.

ESTELLE. Well, not to me.

PAM. On the back of which we ask for our customers to put addresses. Which we keep on file.

Pause.

Everyone is looking at MARGARET.

MARGARET. Um, do you have a phone?

PAM. Of course.

MARGARET. I mean, one I could use. To phone home.

PAM. Ro!

PAM *gestures towards the reception, as* KELLY *goes back to* RAVI.

KELLY. Well, what a drama. To me, Mrs C.

RAVI *wiggles her hands.*

Thank goodness, you and me, we live such uneventful lives.

RAVI. Most uneventful. Yes.

Focus is on to WENDY *and* LYNN *again.* LYNN *is finished and standing.*

LYNN. So how do you know about the Post-Impressionists?

WENDY. My father painted. He based his stuff on Bonnard.

LYNN. Painted?

WENDY. He died last year.

LYNN. I'm sorry.

> *She looks for a tip in her bag.*

> Look . . .

WENDY. You know, when you do someone for a second time, you see the cut. The first cut, from the time before. I always get a real kick from that.

> *Spot on MARGARET, JOEL, RO. MARGARET on the phone. RO grinning helpfully at JOEL.*

MARGARET. Hallo?

> *Lights focus on JULIE with SAMANTHA and KELLY.*

> *JULIE stands.*

JULIE. You know, I've changed my mind. I want my legs done. And I want a manicure. And bugger it.

> *Spot on MARGARET, JOEL and RO.*

MARGARET. Yes dear, it's me.

> *Lights focus on WENDY and LYNN.*

WENDY. Next time, I'll get a real kick from you.

Scene Seven

Hospital Casualty Unit.

Some wounded people are loitering, waiting to be seen. The staff are busy.

PATRICIA and TOM are waiting for ROSE.

PATRICIA. She must have someone.

TOM. No.

PATRICIA. She came to this city alone?

TOM. No. She came with a girlfriend.

PATRICIA. Well then!

TOM. The girlfriend's gone off to Spain. Met a barman who had connections. Rose wasn't so lucky.

PATRICIA. Then she must go back home.

TOM. Some people don't like going home. You should know that.

PATRICIA. Me?

TOM. Yes, you! Why have you never . . .

PATRICIA. Oh don't. Is it still the same?

Everyone used to live in everyone else's kitchens. Just walk in
the back door . . .

TOM. That's right. It's still the same. We're very close like. Very
friendly.

PATRICIA. I didn't find it friendly, I couldn't breathe, Tom.

TOM. It wasn't that bad.

PATRICIA. Not for you maybe! Not for men – down the pit all day,
down the club all night!

TOM. No!

PATRICIA. Yes – even you! Off to choir, off to rugby – I remember!
Every night working for the damned union: 'Sorry Patricia'.

TOM. Listen. You were the only woman . . .

PATRICIA. Don't. Please don't say it . . . I think of you sometimes,
you know.

TOM. Really?

PATRICIA. Whenever I'm selling my soul. I have private
conversations with a man I once knew . . . That's what's so odd
meeting you now. The face had long since gone and then . . .

TOM. In I walk.

PATRICIA. It is good to see you . . .

> *A sudden cacophany as* NGUGI, LEARY, TRISH, BONES,
> AHMED, DEBBIE, SHARON *and* MICHELLE *and others come
> into casualty all talking at once.* NGUGI *is in shock. He has his
> hands crossed in front of him.* LEARIE *carries a fishing rod which
> appears to be attached somehow to* NGUGI.

TRISH (*to* BONES). I'm never going on a boat with you again!

LEARIE. Me neither.

BONES. It's not my fault!

LEARIE (*to* NGUGI). You got to sue him man!

AHMED. You can't sue geese!

LEARIE. The fisherman, dick head!

DEBBIE. Get a solicitor.

MICHELLE. My Dad's got a solicitor.

NURSE. Quiet please! Is someone hurt?

TRISH. He's in shock Nurse.

NURSE. What happened?

BONES. Birmingham won at home.

LEARIE. Shut up Bones – it's no joke!

DEBBIE. He's got a fishing hook stuck right in his . . .

NGUGI. Shut up!

NURSE. Are you all right?

LEARIE. All right? The man is ruined!

NURSE. Come with me.

SHARON. Have you got a bucket?

> *They all follow the* NURSE.

NURSE. Not all of you! (*They ignore her.*) What happened?

SHARON. Well Bones lassoed this goose.

BONES. Perfect shot! And this fisherman on the bank has a blue fit!

LEARIE. Waving his rod at us he was.

MICHELLE. He was raging!

TRISHA. Next thing we know, Ngugi was clutching his . . .

NGUGI. Shut up!

> *They've gone.*

TOM. My God . . . Did you never want children?

PATRICIA. Are you joking?

> *There's a shout from* ROSE *as she comes out with* MARTIN MURPHY.

ROSE. I'm not staying here. Call yourself a doctor? You couldn't doctor a cat!

TOM. Aye aye . . . Rose . . .

ROSE. I'm not stopping here.

MARTIN. She needs bed rest. She should stop in.

ROSE. Thank you, but no.

MARTIN. You're her Aunty I believe?

ROSE. Yes and she'll take care of me thank you very much.

MARTIN. She must have bed rest or she could lose the baby.

ROSE. What do they know?

TOM. Thank you, I'll talk to her . . . Oh Rose . . . Aunty Pat! Ha!

PATRICIA. Very funny. What about going home then Rose?

ROSE. To your place? That's very decent . . .

PATRICIA. No, your home.

ROSE. My home? And where's that? That's where you hang your hat isn't it, home?

TOM. She shouldn't travel.

MARTIN. She mustn't travel.

ROSE. I don't want to travel.

PATRICIA. Then where will you stay?

TOM. She needs some totally unselfish person, I suppose . . .

PATRICIA. Pardon? You're not . . . Oh listen, I have a very small flat . . .

ROSE. Oh that would be wonderful!

PATRICIA. I'm not inviting you . . .

TOM. I only meant as a resting place.

ROSE. I'd be no trouble.

TOM. She's a good girl.

PATRICIA. Oh is she?

ROSE. No, not really. Not in the Biblical sense. But I think you and I would get on!

PATRICIA. Oh . . .

TOM. I think you would.

PATRICIA. Do you indeed? And what would you do – sidle off back to Wales?

TOM. Oh no! No I promise you. Would I leave you expecting a baby?

ROSE. So there you are you see – he'll stop as well!

PATRICIA. I hope I will wake up in the morning and all this will have been a terrible dream . . .

ROSE. Oh, so do I, Patricia, so do I.

They wait for PATRICIA.

She is silent.

TOM. Go on . . . It's why I came back. I've never forgotten this person who really cared . . .

PATRICIA. Not me?

TOM. Of course.

MARTIN. So what are you going to do?

PATRICIA. Come on. I have work to do. Shall we go?

Scene Eight

Dudley Zoo. KIM – *is sitting at a picnic table. Downstage on either side are two couples:* LUIGI BENNEDOTTI *and the Bon Nuit* RECEPTIONIST, TED *and* TRACY.

LUIGI. So then, the giraffes? or sea-lions?

TED. Right. It's the dolphins or koala bears.

RECEPTIONIST. The reptile house?

TRACY. The killer snakes?

LUIGI/TED. OK.

To get to the reptiles and snakes the two couples have to meet. All four cover their faces as best they may and hurry off.

They exit, as all the CHILDREN *come rushing on, to* KIM.

CONNELL. Please! Please ! Please! Please!

ZARA. Can I have a monkey mask?

DANIEL. I want a rubber bat!

KIM. No. You can have an ice cream before we go home. Sit down quietly and wait for the coach.

All the CHILDREN *confer.*

CONNELL. Five minutes!

KIM. One minute.

GABI. Come on.

They all dash off, as RAVI *and* SUE *appear from the opposite direction carrying coffee for* KIM *and each other.*

RAVI. I know the world is changing and for young people it is difficult but my marriage was arranged and we have been very happy.

She hands KIM *the coffee.*

KIM. Thanks.

SUE. How was it arranged?

RAVI. Mish came here from India in 1946. His cousins approached my parents and said we know of a young man for your daughter.

KIM. Oy! Daniel, put that back!

SUE. Did you meet him before the wedding?

RAVI. Oh yes.

SUE. And did you like him?

RAVI (*softening as she remembers*). Oh yes. I thought he was lovely.

KIM. Were you not afraid you would have to spend your whole life with a man you didn't love?

RAVI. I was lucky.

SUE. My husband left me after twenty-three years. Sometimes I think Asian women are fortunate.

RAVI. Well I don't know. I lived with my relatives for seven years before I had a house of my own.

SUE. Women are second class in your culture though – aren't they?

KIM. Connell! Get off that wall – you'll fall in. (*To* RAVI *and* SUE.) All women are second class – not just Asian women.

There is a loud splash, then shouts and cheers of childrens' voices.

KIM. Oh no!

She rushes off.

RAVI. Has someone fallen in the water?

SUE. I hope not.

They both look in the direction of KIM*'s exit and the sound of the splash.*

KIM *reappears.*

KIM. It's OK. A sealion just slid into the pool.

Pause.

I've been married before.

SUE. I never knew that Kim.

KIM. I was the same age as Ravi – I was nineteen.

SUE. And are you courting now or what?

KIM. Courting? I married again. So you see, although we can choose – we can still get it wrong – is what I mean.

All the children appear, they push GABI *forward.*

GABI. The giraffe's got my hat!

ZARA. And mine.

KIM. What happened Daniel?

DANIEL. He's eating Gabi's hat Miss and then Zara threw hers in.

ZARA. No, I didn't.

DANIEL. Yes you did!

SUE. Did you throw your caps in?

IDRIS. No. The giraffe leaned over and took my cap off my head.

ZARA is quietly beating DANIEL *up behind* KIM*'s back.*

KIM (*to* SUE). OK. Come on. All of you.

RAVI. I'll wait for the coach.

> *The children exit with* KIM *and* SUE. RAVI *waits.*

> AAN *approaches.*

RAVI. How did you know where to find me?

AAN. I called at the school, they said you were here.

> RAVI *looks very downcast.*

AAN. She's told you.

RAVI. Aan, I'm so sorry. I had hoped . . .

AAN. Why are you sorry? It's Katya you should apologise to. You've every reason to be proud of her and give her your blessing.

RAVI. To marry an English doctor?

AAN. Yes.

RAVI. What colour will the children be?

AAN. Does it matter?

> RAVI *is upset and wanders away from him.*

RAVI. I always wanted a son. I thought if I had one we'd call him Mahendra. Mahendra Murphy doesn't sound right.

AAN. Aren't there worse things can happen in this country than an Englishman falling in love with your daughter?

RAVI. An Englishman will divorce her in ten years time.

AAN. I see in the eyes of my friends, that not all marriages are happy. I see in their eyes that they would leave if they could.

RAVI. I have those friends too.

AAN. Ravi, I made a decision today – I will come here to study. You will get a son after all.

RAVI (*blows her nose and sniffs to hide emotion*). You're very welcome.

AAN. I think you should see Katya.

RAVI. Mish won't accept it.

AAN. We must arrange a meeting.

> KIM *returns. She has a row of children attached to her by a rope around each of their waists.* SUE *is bringing up the rear.*

KIM (*to* AAN). Have you seen a hippopotamus?

AAN. Has one escaped?

KIM. No. I promised them a hippopotamus before we caught the bus. But I can't find it.

    RAVI *gets out her map of the zoo.*

RAVI. Hang on. No 48. I think I can find it.

AAN. Can I come with you?

KIM. Sure. We could do with another pair of hands.

    AAN *helps* RAVI *collect lunch boxes and coats and push chairs and follows the troop off in search of a hippopotamus.*

RAVI. According to this it's right next to the sealions. Up the hill, turn right.

    They exit.

CONNELL. What do hippopotamuses do?

Scene Nine

Landing of a high-rise.

MARGARET, JOEL *and* NORMAN *have arrived outside a particular flat door.*

MARGARET. Well. Number 15. Here we are.

    Pause.

NORMAN. Well. Ring the bell, then, Margaret.

MARGARET. On the evidence so far, I doubt if it'll work.

NORMAN. Well, bang the door.

    Pause.

MARGARET. I'm nervous now.

NORMAN. Oh, that'll be the day.

    MARGARET *looks at* NORMAN. *The door opens.* RITA BRACEBRIDGE *stands there.*

RITA. Uh – can I help you?

MARGARET. Miss Bracebridge?

RITA. Yes.

MARGARET. We understand you know someone we're looking for.

RITA. Go on.

MARGARET. Her name is Sandra Price.

Pause.

RITA. And who are you?

MARGARET. Do you know where she is – staying?

RITA. I'll repeat the question. Who are you?

MARGARET. I am her mother.

Pause.

RITA. Are you now?

Pause.

Well, she is – staying here.

Pause.

And at the moment she is down at my allotment. Doing amazing things to leeks.

MARGARET. And where is your allotment?

Pause. RITA goes into the flat.

She reappears with a gardening basket.

RITA. Follow me.

Scene Ten

The balcony or roof garden of PATRICIA'*s flat. It has a panoramic view of the city.*

ROSE *comes on pursued by* PATRICIA.

PATRICIA. Rose!

ROSE. Don't shout at me, I'll lose the baby! You shout and I'll jump!

PATRICIA. I'm not shouting at you, and I'm not throwing you out, but if you stay here, there will have to be rules! Now come inside!

TOM *comes out.*

TOM. For the baby's sake Rose . . . you must stop smoking!

PATRICIA. Rule number one!

ROSE. I'm not smoking! You can't call these titchy things cigarettes!

PATRICIA. And I don't mind you using the phone . . .

ROSE. I was only ordering things for the baby! You know, Uncle, with this book, you can buy everything you want in the world just by picking up the phone! You need never leave the flat!

PATRICIA. But it's not free Rose – that number you gave them – it means that I pay.

ROSE. I'll pay you back, honest I will!

PATRICIA. It won't work!

TOM. I'll pay.

PATRICIA. This is not going to work.

ROSE. My God, you've got a wonderful view from up here . . .

PATRICIA. What?

TOM. It is. You can see the whole city.

PATRICIA. Yes. Yes and in case you get bored, they build something new every day. It is marvellous.

ROSE. Just like Dallas!

TOM. The Wild West.

PATRICIA. Too wild, I'm sorry I have to have order. I have to work Rose . . .

ROSE. Not at home?

PATRICIA. Yes, I work from home and I need . . .

ROSE. Oww!

PATRICIA. Don't you dare!

ROSE. No, it's all right, it's only kicking. Tom get me the

stethoscope. Come and have a listen.

Go on . . . it's beautiful.

PATRICIA. Listen to what?

ROSE. You can hear its little heart beating.

TOM *offers the stethoscope.*

TOM. Here . . .

PATRICIA *listens.*

PATRICIA. Where did you get this?

ROSE. Under the gooseberry bush. Where d'you think?

PATRICIA. The stethoscope.

ROSE. I've borrowed it from the hospital.

PATRICIA. I can hear it!

TERRY *comes in.*

TERRY. Here you are!

PATRICIA. My God! Come and listen to this . . .

ROSE. That's it – roll up, roll up! Only tenpence a listen – hear the heart beating! Come along now!

TERRY *listens. They are all crouched around* ROSE.

ROSE. So my little one – you're going to be born in Birmingham . . .

Can you hear it now?

JOHAN *passes by at ground level.*

Scene Eleven

Allotments near park.

We can see the playground area. People are working their allotments. RITA, MARGARET, JOEL *and* NORMAN *arrive.*

RITA. Well, here we are.

MARGARET. So where is she?

RITA. Hey, Sandra!

> SANDRA *is on her knees, facing upstage. She doesn't turn round, but calls back.*

SANDRA. Yuh?

RITA. Guess who?

> SANDRA *turns on her knees. She looks at her mother and father. She doesn't move.*

SANDRA. Oh. Christ.

MARGARET. Hallo there, darling.

SANDRA. Oh. Oh, bloody hell.

> *She stands and comes over. As she does so:*

(*To* RITA). Oh, why on earth . . .

RITA. What else was I supposed to do?

MARGARET. Sandra, who is this woman? Why are you living with her?

SANDRA. I found her.

MARGARET. What, you just stumbled . . .

SANDRA. No. I was looking for her.

MARGARET. Looking for her, why? Who is she?

SANDRA. She's my mother.

> *Pause.*

MARGARET. Your real mother's dead.

SANDRA. No she isn't. She's right here. In her allotment.

> *Pause.* MARGARET *turns to* NORMAN.

MARGARET. How did she know? *How did she know?*

NORMAN. I . . . I . . .

MARGARET. Just tell me *how she knew.*

SANDRA. You didn't tell her? *Dad.*

MARGARET. He'll tell me now.

> *Pause.*

NORMAN. Well, I . . .

SANDRA. Don't you remember? In the kitchen? Because I
remember every single word.

Pause.

– (*Prompting.*) 'You see, Sandra, what we can't understand, is
why you're so incapable of gratitude.'

Slight pause.

– Go on, Dad. Say it.

NORMAN. 'You see, what we can't understand, is why you're so
incapable of gratitude.'

SANDRA. 'You know, Dad, if I'm such a nightmare to you, I don't
know why you took me on at all. If I'm such a burden. Such a
nightmare.'

Pause.

NORMAN. 'Well, we adopted you because we wanted you to have a
proper, normal life.'

SANDRA. 'You call this normal?'

Pause.

NORMAN. 'But if we're so impossible, if it's so terrible to live with
us, if we're so – what was your word – "authoritarian", if we're
actually, what did you say, "just bloody fascists", then . . . then
you can always go back. If you want to. Go back to your real
mother. See what she can do.'

Pause.

SANDRA. 'My real mother's dead. Or so – or so you told me.'

Pause.

MARGARET. Norman.

SANDRA. Lies. All throughout my life. Lies. Lies. About who I am.
About where I come from. I mean, I wonder. I do wonder,
what kind of people you are. To be able to – to tell so many
lies.

She runs off.

NORMAN. Sandra . . .

He runs off after her. MARGARET *doesn't know what to do.*

MARGARET. Oh, Joel. Joel, What do I do now?

JOEL. Tell them the truth.

MARGARET. What truth?

JOEL. The truth about why you couldn't have a baby of your own.

> MARGARET *is speechless.* JOEL *takes her by the shoulders.*

> Go on Margaret. 'If a job's worth starting, it's worth finishing.' Show a bit of gumption. Bit of guts. Will there ever be a better time?

> *Pause.*

> *Then* MARGARET *squares her shoulders. She turns and walks out after her husband and adopted daughter.*

> *A moment between* JOEL *and* RITA.

JOEL. How did she find you?

RITA. Well, she knew her birthday. And they'd told her that she'd been born here. Just – thank God I never married.

JOEL. Sorry?

RITA. Kept the name.

> *Slight pause.*

> And how did you meet up with her?

JOEL. I was picked up at the bus station.

RITA. While arriving or departing?

JOEL. Well, in theory I was going to Jamaica.

RITA. And in practice?

> *Pause.*

JOEL. I dunno.

RITA. Well. There they are.

> *They look over to the playground area. We see* NORMAN, MARGARET *and* SANDRA *enter and sit on the bench.* JOEL *and* RITA *look at each other and decide to go over to them.*

> MARGARET *sits between* NORMAN *and* SANDRA. *They are facing away from each other.* JOEL *and* RITA *come up to them.*

> *There is a moment before* MARGARET *speaks.*

MARGARET. You know. When I arrived here, at the bus station, there were three people, who had come here, to the city, to look for people who they'd lost. And I'd really like to know, I really would, what the others found. Because I have found what I was looking for. But I've also – found out what it was. And although it was . . . It wasn't.

Pause.

If you see what I mean.

She looks up at JOEL.

But I have to tell you, what I've found, what I've found out I was looking for, I could not have found, without . . .

Pause.

Understanding that a threefold cord is not so quickly broken.

JOEL *goes to* MARGARET *and puts out his hand.*

JOEL. Hey, come on.

MARGARET. Come on what?

JOEL. Come where. Come here.

MARGARET *takes* JOEL's *hand and allows herself to be led to the slide.*

Go on.

MARGARET. Oh Joel.

JOEL. Go on, Mrs P. Just show them the extent of your regression. Like I mean, I think it's like pretty damned important that they know.

A pause.

MARGARET *climbs the ladder. She sits on the slide. She slides down. She remains seated at the bottom of the slide.*

JOEL. You see?

SANDRA *stands, goes and sits next to her mother on the bottom of the slide. She takes her hands. A moment.*

Then NORMAN *follows. He puts his hands on* MARGARET's *shoulders.*

(*To* RITA). They see.

Lights fade on the family and RITA. JOEL *walks forward. We hear the* INSPECTOR *and the* DEPUTY INSPECTOR:

INSPECTOR. Attention. The 20.15 hours for Leicester Derby Sheffield Leeds and Newcastle departs from Bay Fourteen.

DEPUTY INSPECTOR. Attention please. All passengers for the twenty hundred Air Express should now be boarding at Bay Ten.

JOEL *takes a bus ticket from his wallet. He looks at it.*

INSPECTOR. The coach arriving at Bay Seven is the 14.30 hours from Bangor, Llangollen, Oswestry, Shrewsbury and Wolverhampton.

DEPUTY INSPECTOR. Bay Ten the last call to Heathrow.

JOEL *tears up the ticket and goes out.*

Scene Twelve

Diwalli.

The Hindu temple is thronged with people lighting candles and sitting in groups in different parts of the temple. Two drums, cymbals, and accordion and bells can be heard.

MARTIN MURPHY *and* KATYA *have just entered.*
KATYA (*explaining*). Lakshmi is the Goddess of Wealth.

MARTIN. It's like Christmas!

KATYA. No. Diwalli is our New Year.

MARTIN. What about the God with the elephant's head? What's his name . . .

KATYA. Gunesh.

MARTIN. He's my favourite god.

KATYA. Gunesh removes obstacles and ensures success.

MARTIN. Why do we leave our shoes outside – is it just hygiene?

KATYA. No. It's believed that you leave the everyday world with your shoes at the door.

MARTIN. Why only the shoes?

KATYA *laughs.*

KATYA. Thank you for coming with me.

MARTIN. I feel quite at home. All these candles remind me of my childhood.

 KATYA *goes towards the shrine where the biggest throng of people are.*

MARTIN. What will happen?

KATYA. The ceremony is called Arti – it happens twice a day.

MARTIN. Katya – isn't that Pushba?

 RAVI *and* MISH *follow* AAN *towards* KATYA, *leaving* PUSHBA *with friends.*

KATYA. Mother . . .

 KATYA *panics and turns to flee, but* MARTIN *blocks her way.*

MARTIN. No don't go.

AAN (*smiling*). Hello Martin.

MARTIN. Hello Aan.

 They shake hands.

AAN. I want to introduce Katya's parents, Mish and Ravi.

 MARTIN *very courteously puts his palms and fingertips together as if to pray and bows his head as a greeting.*

AAN. This is Martin Murphy.

KATYA. I was just explaining the Arti ceremony.

AAN. Please go on.

KATYA. The water which is used to bathe the images is then sprinkled over the congregation.

MARTIN. What are the flowers for?

KATYA. Flowers are passed around so that we can ask the God to guide our actions.

MARTIN. May I join in?

KATYA. Of course you must.

RAVI. You must also eat the Prashda when it is passed around.

MARTIN. Prashda?

KATYA. Sweetmeats.

MISH. You see how they circle the lights in front of the images.

MARTIN. Can we go in closer?

MISH. Yes. Of course.

> MARTIN *goes forward with* AAN *and* KATYA, *while* MISH *drops back to* RAVI. RAVI *beckons* PUSHBA *to join them.*

RAVI. He seems a nice boy.

MISH. Mahendra Murphy?

RAVI. I'm getting used to it.

PUSHBA. What if she has a girl?

MISH. No more girls. Girls are too much trouble. We must ask Gunesh.

> *They all go off towards the shrine to worship, leaving* PUSHBA.

PUSHBA. I shall ask Gunesh for something too. I have plenty of time when he comes here to study. I'll watch him every day. And then in three or four years maybe – he'll look up one day and notice me. He might even find he is in love with me. And of course, I shall be terribly surprised.

AAN (*voice off-stage*). Pushba!

> AAN *comes out of the crowd looking for her.*

AAN. Pushba!

PUSHBA. You see. It's started.

Scene Thirteen

The candles, drums, cymbals, accordions and bells of the Diwalli; but changing.

The candles begin to move, the circle around the shrine becomes a procession, joined by performers with more candles, bells and lanterns. The Hindu music is changing too: we recognise the Coventry Carol.

In short, the ritual of the Diwalli is turning into Christmas.

ALL.

Coventry Carol

Lully, lullay,
thou little tiny child,
By by, lully lullay.

O sisters too,
How may we do
For to preserve this day
This poor youngling
For whom we do sing,
By by, lully, lullay?

Herod the king,
In his raging,
Charged he hath this day
His men of might,
In his own sight,
All young children to slay.

That woe is me,
Poor child for thee!
And ever morn and day,
For thy parting
Neither say nor sing
By by, lully lullay!

In the midst of the singing, we catch glimpses of our main characters:
AAN, KATYA*'s family,* MARTIN *and* KATYA; NORMAN,
MARGARET *and* SANDRA; RITA *and* JOEL.

RAVI. And while Aan found his place at university,

SANDRA. And Rita a small place for Sandra,

MARTIN. And Katya her new place in her parents' lives . . .

KATYA. Not too near,

RITA. But not too far . . .

MARGARET. And as Norman took a month off work,

NORMAN. And he and Margaret went on holiday,

SANDRA. Apart,

NORMAN. But came back rather more together . . .

JOEL. And as Joel finally decided that you're ultimately closer to the place you live in than the place from whence you came . . .

PUSHBA. So someone else . . .

AAN. Somewhere in Birmingham . . .

MARGARET. Was proving nonetheless that it can be pretty damned important where you're born.

Then, through the procession, comes a woman in a mac with car keys; meeting a man carrying a suitcase and a younger woman carrying a baby.

The woman with the car keys is PATRICIA; *she has come to meet* TOM, ROSE *and the baby, out of hospital.*

In the middle of all the celebration and mystery, there is a prosaic little moment of dispute about who is carrying the suitcase and who the baby.

And then this unlikely trio – or rather, with the baby, this unlikely quartet – become aware that they are the centre of attention, of the procession and the audience. Like a rabbit caught in the headlamps of a car, they are frozen into a state of confused but polite bemusement: a successful businesswoman, an elderly Welshman, a young woman he picked up in a bus station, her three-day old child, in the middle of the city, on Christmas Eve, surrounded by the rising strains of a favourite carol, and then, finally, by the darkness.

ALL. O sisters too
How may we do
For to preserve this day
This poor youngling
For whom we sing
By by, lully, lullay.

End